A CIRCLE OF QUIET

Also by Madeleine L'Engle

The Crosswicks Journal
BOOK 1

A Circle of Quiet

Madeleine L'Engle

The Seabury Press • New York

Fourth printing

The Seabury Press
815 Second Avenue
New York, N.Y. 10017

Copyright © 1972 by Madeleine L'Engle Franklin

Published 1972 by Farrar, Straus and Giroux
Seabury paperback edition 1979

Library of Congress Catalog Card Number: 79-65524
ISBN: 0-8164-2260-5

Printed in the United States of America

This book is for Charlotte Rebecca Jones

ONE

We are four generations under one roof this summer, from infant Charlotte to almost-ninety Great-grandmother. This is a situation which is getting rarer and rarer in this day and age when families are divided by large distances and small dwellings. Josephine and Alan and the babies come from England; Great-grandmother from the Deep South; Hugh and I and our younger children from New York; and our assorted "adopted" children from as far afield as Mexico and as close as across the road; all to be together in Crosswicks, our big, old-fashioned New England farmhouse. It's an ancient house by American standards—well over two hundred years old. It still seems old to me, although Josephine and Alan, in Lincoln, live close by the oldest inhabited house in Europe, built in the eleven-hundreds.

When our children were little and we lived in Crosswicks year round, they liked to count things. They started to count the books, but stopped after they got to three thousand. They also counted beds, and figured that as long as all the double beds held two people, we could sleep twenty-one; that, of course, included the attic. We are using the attic this summer, though we haven't yet slept twenty-one. A lot of the time it is twelve, and even more to feed. Cooking is the only part of housekeeping I manage with any grace; it's something like writing a book: you look in the refrigerator and see what's there, choose all the ingredients you need, and a few your husband thinks you don't need, and put them all together to concoct a dish. Vacuum cleaners are simply something more for me to trip over; and a kitchen floor, no matter how grubby, looks better before I wax it. The sight of a meal's worth of dirty dishes, pots, and pans makes me want to run in the other direction. Every so often I need OUT; something will throw me into total disproportion, and I have to get away from everybody—away from all these people I love most in the world—in order to regain a sense of proportion.

I like hanging sheets on lines strung under the apple trees— the birds like it, too. I enjoy going out to the incinerator after dark and watching the flames; my bad feelings burn away with the trash. But the house is still visible, and I can hear the sounds from within; often I need to get away completely, if only for a few minutes. My special place is a small brook in a green glade, a circle of quiet from which there is no visible sign of human beings. There's a natural stone bridge over the brook, and I sit there, dangling my legs and looking through the foliage at the sky reflected in the water, and things slowly come back into perspective. If the insects are biting me—and they usually are; no place is quite perfect—I use the pliable branch of a shadblow tree as a fan. The brook wanders through a tunnel of foliage, and the birds sing more sweetly there than anywhere else; or perhaps it is just that when I am at the brook I have time to be aware of them, and I move slowly into a kind of peace that is marvelous, "annihilating all that's made to a green thought in a green shade." If I sit for a while, then my impatience, crossness, frustration, are indeed annihilated, and my sense of humor returns.

It's a ten-minute walk to the brook. I cross the lawn and go through the willow tree which splashes its fountain of green down onto the grass so that it's almost impossible to mow

4

around it. If it's raining and I really need the brook badly, I go in my grandfather's old leather hunting coat and a strange yellow knitted hat from Ireland (one of my children, seeing me set off, asked, "Who do you think you are, Mother? Mrs Whatsit?"); it's amazing what passing the half-century mark does to free one to be eccentric. When my hair gets wet I look like a drowned ostrich, and I much prefer resembling an amiable, myopic giraffe as I wade through the wet clover of the large pasture. It's already been hayed twice this summer: does the neighboring farmer, who uses our pastures in addition to his own, hay clover? I was born in the middle of the asphalt island of Manhattan, and even nearly a decade of living in Crosswicks all year round has not made me conversant with bucolic terms. When Hugh and I bought the house the spring after we were married (we walked into a run-down place that hadn't been loved for years, and it opened its arms to us) and I saw cows in the pasture, they didn't look like cows to me. My idea of cows was from illustrations in children's books.

After the pasture is traversed, I walk through a smaller pasture which has been let go to seed because of all the rocks, and is now filled with thistles. Then there is a stone wall to be climbed; the only poison ivy around here grows on and by the stones of this wall, and I'm trying to kill it by smothering it with wet Sunday *Times*es; my children have made me very aware of the danger of using chemical sprays. Perhaps I've discovered a new use for *The New York Times?* (We also use it for the cats.) I think the poison ivy is less flourishing than it was; at any rate *The New York Times* is not going to unbalance the ecology. I love the *ology* words; *ology*: the word about. *Eco*, man's dwelling place. The word about where man lives.

Once I'm over the stone wall, the terrain changes. I step into a large field full of rocks left from glacial deposits; there are many ancient apple trees which, this summer, are laden with fruit. From the stone wall to the brook takes two balls of twine. Unreliable eyes make my vision variable, and there are days when my string path is extremely helpful, although, as my husband remarks, "All anybody who wants to find your secret hideout needs to do is climb the stone wall and follow the string."

That's all right. All secret places need to be shared occasionally. So the string guides me across a high ridge where there are large outcroppings of glacial stone, including our special star-watching rock. Then the path becomes full of tussocks and hummocks; my legs are etched by the thorns of blackberry brambles and wild roses. Earlier this summer the laurel burst from snow into fire, and a few weeks later we found a field of sweet wild strawberries. And then there are blueberry bushes, not very many, but a few, taller than I am and, to me, infinitely beautiful.

The burning bush: somehow I visualize it as much like one of these blueberry bushes. The bush burned, was alive with flame and was not consumed. Why? Isn't it because, as a bush, it was perfect? It was exactly as a bush is meant to be. A bush certainly doesn't have the opportunity for prideful and selfish choices, for self-destruction, that we human beings do. It *is*. It is a pure example of ontology. Ecology—ontology—the words fascinate me. Ontology is one of my son-in-law's favorite words, and I'm apt to get drunk on words, to go on jags; ontology is my jag for this summer, and I'm grateful to Alan for it—as for so much else. Ontology: the word about the essence of things; the word about being.

I go to the brook because I get out of being, out of the essential. So I'm not like the bush, then. I put all my prickliness, selfishness, in-turnedness, onto my *is*ness; we all tend to, and when we burn, this part of us is consumed. When I go past the tallest blueberry bush, where my twine is tied to one of the branches, I think that the part of us that has to be burned away is something like the deadwood on the bush; it has to go, to be burned in the terrible fire of reality, until there is nothing left but our ontological selves; what we are meant to be.

I go to the brook and my tensions and frustrations are lost as I spend a happy hour sitting right in the water and trying to clear it of the clogging debris left by a fallen tree.

.. 2 ..

Still damp, with fingernails broken and dirty, and a few extra scratches on my legs, I return to the house and go up to my Private Workroom. When Hugh and I bought Crosswicks, this room, which is over the garage, was used for chickens. The garage is even older than the house, having originally been the first trading post on the old Indian Trail. It was turned into a garage about ten years before we came. There were still strips of wallpaper downstairs with the car and upstairs with the chicken coops. When we moved in, the chickens were gone but the floor was covered with hay and chicken droppings—marvelous for Hugh's garden, and we shoveled this organic fertilizer out the window.

It was almost fifteen years before we were able to turn it into my study, and it was supposed to be Absolutely Private. Nobody was allowed up without special invitation. The children called it the Ivory Tower, and it is still called the Tower, though it is neither ivory nor private nor, in fact, tower.

This summer Alan has taken it over for his doctoral thesis. I am privileged to have him read me the first draft, and to offer occasional suggestions as to syntax and construction. I tell him about the blueberry bush and my thoughts about the burning bush, and he turns to his thesis where he reads me a quotation from Sartre about the *isness* of an oak tree; but Sartre felt depressed and threatened by this; the idea that the oak tree simply *is* seemed to diminish him. I suppose the perfect *isness* of anything would be frightening without the hope of God. An oak tree is, and it doesn't matter to it—at least Sartre thinks it doesn't; it is not a thinking oak. Man is; it matters to him; this is terrifying unless it matters to God, too, because this is the only possible reason we can matter to ourselves: not because we are sufficient unto ourselves—I am not: my husband, my family, my friends give me my meaning and, in a sense, my being, so that I know that I, like the burning bush, or the oak tree, am ontological: essential: real.

. . 3 . .

For the last two weeks of July this summer I abandoned the family, the kitchen stove, the brook, and flew out to Ohio State University to be Writer in Residence for a special program of Reading Fellows. It was a completely different world from the community of Crosswicks, and yet it too was community, and there were many aspects of each which overlapped and intertwined.

I learned, a good many years ago, that it is impossible for me to have a seminar in writing practices without coming to care deeply about my students. I may, and do, remain objective about their writing, but I am committed to them as persons. And I learn from them probably more than they learn from me. During those two tight-packed weeks at O.S.U. I lived, worked, ate with about twenty-five young men and women from all over the United States, who had already had teaching experience and who had been together for a full year of intensive reading and study. I was with them for their final two weeks. The first night, Dr. Charlotte Huck and Dr. Martha King took me out to dinner. They had never had a Writer in Residence before. I had never been a Writer in Residence before. We sat in an elegant roof-top restaurant which looked out over all of Columbus, and I, hoping to be able to relax and enjoy my dinner, asked, "Just exactly what do you want me to do, these two weeks?"

Martha took a calm sip of her Old-fashioned. "I was hoping it would emerge."

It did. I had brought a lot of notes, and the morning session was a general lecture and discussion, while the afternoon session was a sort of crash course in writing practices, with specific daily writing assignments. I had expected, during the question periods after both morning and afternoon sessions, that I would get questions about writing, and teaching children something about the arts; mostly I got questions about the nature of the universe. Perhaps the questions weren't as direct as those I get from high-school or grade-school students, because these men and women were experienced and sophisticated; but their queries were aimed in the same direction.

In the beginning we were all a little tentative with each other, as though we were going into a cold lake, and testing the water first. I knew that these students, most with master's degrees, and many on their way to Ph.D.'s—or, as Alan rather casually says, Phids—knew far more about theories of education than I do, and yet I had been asked to talk to them about creativity, and teaching creativity to children. The first morning I decided that we'd never get anywhere if I worried about getting my feet wet.

They were a varied group, as varied as our Crosswicks community. Their age ranged from early twenties to late forties. They were black, white, yellow; there were Roman Catholic nuns, a lay preacher from the Christian Church, Southern Baptists, agnostics, atheists. Therefore, there was a certain difference in our vocabulary; I wanted to be very careful that when we used a word everybody would understand it in the same way, and this meant that we did a lot of stopping to define. Often I would use a word which I hoped did not already have a preconditioned meaning for them. Ontology, for instance. It was a legitimate excuse to use my word-for-the-summer, and it's a word that has a lot to do with creativity and teaching.

It was the first time that I'd been forced to think consciously about creativity in connection with little children, rather than the older ones for whom I often write. I was trying to think out loud about the concentration essential for all artists, and in the very little child I found the perfect example. The concentration of a small child at play is analogous to the concentration of the artist of any discipline. In real play, which is real concentration, the child is not only outside time, he is outside *himself*. He has thrown himself completely into whatever it is that he is doing. A child playing a game, building a sand castle, painting a picture, is completely *in* what he is doing. His *self*-consciousness is gone; his consciousness is wholly focused outside himself.

I had just witnessed this in Crosswicks, observing an eighteen-month-old lying on her stomach on the grass watching a colony of ants, watching with total, spontaneous concentration. And I had played ring-around-a-rosy with her; we skipped around in a circle, grandparents, parents, assorted teenagers, wholly outside ourselves, holding hands, falling in abandon onto the lawn, joining in the child's shrieks of delighted laughter.

And with her we were outside self and outside time.

When we are *self*-conscious, we cannot be wholly aware; we must throw ourselves out first. This throwing ourselves away is the act of creativity. So, when we wholly concentrate, like a child in play, or an artist at work, then we share in the act of creating. We not only escape time, we also escape our self-conscious selves.

The Greeks had a word for ultimate self-consciousness which I find illuminating: *hubris*: pride: pride in the sense of putting oneself in the center of the universe. The strange and terrible thing is that this kind of total self-consciousness invariably ends in self-annihilation. The great tragedians have always understood this, from Sophocles to Shakespeare. We witness it in history in such people as Tiberius, Eva Perón, Hitler.

I was timid about putting forth most of these thoughts, but this kind of timidity is itself a form of pride. The moment that humility becomes self-conscious, it becomes hubris. One cannot be humble and aware of oneself at the same time. Therefore, the act of creating—painting a picture, singing a song, writing a story—is a humble act? This was a new thought to me. Humility is throwing oneself away in complete concentration on something or someone else.

I remember learning to skip rope. It's not too difficult when you hold the rope yourself. But then there's learning to jump into a rope swung by two other children, learning to jump in without breaking the rhythm and tripping over the rope. It can't be done unless you have that special kind of creative courage which is unself-conscious: the moment you wonder whether or not you can do it, you can't.

So, talking to that diverse group of students in July, I jumped in, as I had finally learned to jump into the rhythm of the curving rope.

Creativity is an act of discovering. The very small child, the baby, is still unself-conscious enough to take joy in discovering himself: he discovers his fingers; he gives them his complete, unself-conscious concentration. Self-conscious adults have done great damage by their misunderstanding—for instance, their attitude towards the child discovering his genitals. Unless the child has been taught corruption incredibly early, this is an unself-conscious discovery of himself, a humble joy of discovery, bearing no resemblance whatsoever to self-conscious auto-eroticism. We, as adults, often fall into perversity in other areas of discovery: i.e., some modern (and not so modern) art in all forms, where the artist is concentrating more on himself than on his painting or music or story. I would venture a guess that an artist concentrating wholly unself-consciously, wholly thrown into his work, is incapable of producing pornography. All perversion is self-gratification. In true love, the lover's pleasure comes in giving himself wholly to the loved one. When we try to give ourselves to ourselves, that is not only perversion, it is ultimately suicide.

A writer may be self-conscious about his work before and after but not during the writing. If I am self-conscious during the actual writing of a scene, then it ends up in the round file. All those rejected chapters, those reams of paper: am I helping to unbalance the ecology?

The kind of unself-consciousness I'm thinking about becomes clearer to me when I turn to a different discipline: for instance, that of playing a Bach fugue at the piano, precisely because I will never be a good enough pianist to play a Bach fugue as it should be played. But when I am actually sitting at the piano, all there is for me is the music. I am wholly in it, unless I fumble so badly that I perforce become self-conscious. Mostly, no matter how inadequate my playing, the music is all that matters: I am outside time, outside self, in play, in joy. When we can play with the unself-conscious concentration of a child, this is: art: prayer: love.

When I talk to any kind of a group, it works only if I throw myself wholly outside of myself and into the job. I may—and do—go through pride, anxiety, inadequacy beforehand, and perhaps after, but not during. The work itself knocks me out of the way. When, as sometimes happens, I am given an overdose of praise, my conscious mind is at first startled, jolted, and then it simply swats the words away, like a fly, a biting fly: it knows such words are dangerous.

And yet—I remember these honey-sweet words, and this remembering itself is vain. Ah, surely it is vain to think about words of praise. It is permissible for us to be pleased that a job has been well done, but we can't take any personal credit for it. We can only be grateful that the work itself knocks self-consciousness out of the way, for it is only thus that the work can be done.

. . 4 . .

The first thing I tried to do was to learn their names. To be known by name is terribly important, though I tend, as usual, to carry my feeling for the name to disproportionate lengths. There is nothing more frightening, for instance, than being a patient in a hospital where you are a number and a case first, and a person second, if at all.

And then there's Emily Brontë . . .

One day, a summer ago, I paid our grocery bill for the month. Our new checkbook was with my husband in the city, but I had a rather elderly checkbook which did not have the mandatory cybernetic salad in the bottom left-hand corner. However, I had the money in the bank, and I had my right and proper signature on the check. I was brought up to believe that, if I need to, I can use a piece of birch bark, write in the name of the bank, the person to whom the money is to go, the sum, the signature, and this constitutes a valid check.

But my check bounced. When it was explained to me that this was because it was missing some magnetic gibberish, I was furious. I was furious at the dinner table, furious so loudly that my husband was forced to bang on the table and shout at me to shut up.

I shut up. But I didn't forget it. Everything I feel about names, about ontology, really, had been violated. Then, at Christmastime, a friend bought something for me, and I reached for a check to repay him the ten dollars and fifty cents. Because I have both French Huguenot and Scots blood I am stubborn and frugal: I saw no reason why my old checks weren't still valid, and I wasn't about to waste them.

My friend said, "Oh, come off it, Madeleine, you know that check won't go through."

His job is to handle vast sums of money daily; he knows what he's talking about. I asked, "Do you really and truly mean that my signature, my *name*, means nothing, absolutely nothing at all?"

"That's what I mean."

It was a wet and windy day. I looked at the rain slashing against the windows, pulled out a check with cybernetic salad in the bottom left-hand corner, said, "All right, then, I feel like Emily Brontë today," and signed it *Emily Brontë*.

My friend was not amused. "Madeleine, what are you doing?"

"You just told me that my name means nothing, absolutely nothing at all. Okay, so I feel like Emily Brontë and I don't see why I shouldn't sign it Emily Brontë. Take it—just for fun—and let's see what happens."

"I know perfectly well what's going to happen. I won't get my money."

But after lunch he came in, looking rather sheepish. He had his ten dollars and fifty cents, and no questions asked at the bank about the signature. "But it won't go through with your monthly statement. It'll bounce."

"All right. If it bounces I'll write you another check."

It did not bounce. I now have cancelled checks signed Emily Brontë, Jane Austen, and Elizabeth Barrett Browning.

In the battle between Madeleine and the machine, at this point the machine is winning.

.. 5 ..

A signature; a name; the very being of the person you talk to, the child you teach, is at stake.

One day during the morning session at Ohio State, Yetta said, "We have to give the child a self-image."

Yetta (it means "The given," and surely Yetta is a gift) is from Alabama. She is black, and gentle, with a core of steel; she has much to be bitter about, and angry; but she also knows how to love. When she said that about the self-image, I stopped her. "Hold everything, Yetta. All my little red warning flags are out. I sniff danger here. Do we want to give the child an *image* of himself—mirror vision? Or do we want what is real?"

That stopped us all. Nobody had thought very much before

about the repercussions in the words: self-image: it's part of the jargon. But I was concerned that we use such words and phrases carefully, knowing precisely what we meant.

What is a self-image? Who started talking about one? I rather fancy it was Madison Avenue. Picture Satan in a business suit, with well-groomed horns and a superbly switching tail, sitting at his huge executive's desk, thinking, "Aha! If I can substitute images for reality I can get a lot more people under my domination."

Do I exaggerate? Possibly. Nevertheless, I am honestly unhappy about Madison Avenue. The advertiser is in business to sell his product to as many people as possible. We forget that most successful high-pressure advertising campaigns deal subtly with our weaknesses, our insecure longing for status (I've never quite overcome my yearning to earn a Merit Badge as a housewife), so that we are being manipulated. A pitch to make us buy a new car or a new stove when our old one is perfectly good, so that we'll have a better "image" of ourselves, doesn't make sense, but it's what the advertiser's in business for. And the powers of darkness know exactly where to infiltrate.

Give the public the "image" of what it thinks it ought to be, or what television commercials or glossy magazine ads have convinced us we ought to be, and we will buy more of the product, become closer to the image, and further from reality.

But what is a true image? *Imagination* comes from "image." An image is not in itself intrinsically wrong. What is true real? Can an image be ontological? The medieval mystics say that the true image and the true real met once and for all on the cross: once and for all: and yet they still meet daily.

And what does all this mean in an un-air-conditioned classroom in Columbus, Ohio, on a hot morning in late July?

It's not a question to be settled either by saints or by Satan. It is something absolutely essential to a writer. Imagery is one of the writer's chief tools. Where would we be without the images given in metaphor and simile?

Metaphor: *She speaks poniards, and every word stabs.* Simile: *My love is like a red, red rose.* "Like" is our simile word. Madison Avenue is by no means the first to misuse "like," but I was told that the man who wrote the famous "Winston tastes good like a cigarette should" did it with contempt for those at whom the commercial was aimed. Over and over again we hear "like" misused this way: *I feel like I'm going to throw up; well, you know, Mother, like I really do need it because . . . ; tell it like it is.* Every time "like" is misused, it is weakened as a simile word.

I'm not against changes in the language. I love new words, and not only the ologies. I've just discovered "widdershins": against the direction of the sun. In Crosswicks the bath water runs out clockwise; in Australia, widdershins. I love anything that is going to make language richer and stronger. But when words are used in a way that is going to weaken language, it has nothing to do with the beautiful way that they can wriggle and wiggle and develop and enrich our speech, but instead it is impoverishing, diminishing. If our language is watered down, then mankind becomes less human, and less free—though we may buy more of the product.

So. An image is something that helps us catch a glimpse of reality. A poet, a storyteller, could not work without images. Nevertheless, an image is only an image, a reflection not unlike the reflections of the shadows of reality in Plato's cave.

If an image is not easy to define, an icon is even more difficult. We usually think of icons as corrupt images which ought to be broken. But it is only the icon misused (like *"like"* misused) which needs breaking. A true icon is not a reflection; it is like a metaphor, a different, *unlike* look at something, and carries within it something of that at which it looks. In Russia or Greece, when a painter begins to learn about icons, he is taught that the icon must never look *like* the person it portrays, it must never be an attempt at a photographic likeness, otherwise it becomes only an image. An icon, if it "works," is more than itself; it bears a fragment of reality.

Red flags of danger again: it is precisely because an icon touches on reality that it far too often becomes an idol. All of us who need icons—and I am convinced that all artists do—also need an iconoclast close by. I'm lucky: my husband is an iconoclast par excellence.

The idea that an icon must not look like the person it portrays used to bother me. But my husband is an actor; there are many times when he has to be away, on an out-of-town tryout of a play, for instance. And I have found that the longer we have been married, and the more deeply I love him, the less I "see" him visually. "Close your eyes," I'm in the habit of telling my students of all ages, "and think about the person you love most in the world. Do you really see him visually? Or don't you see on a much deeper level? It's lots easier to visualize people we don't know very well."

I've noticed in many of my favorite novels that the minor characters are more minutely described, much more physical detail is given about them, than about the hero. A protagonist should be an icon for the reader. A photograph can be a simile, an image; it can seldom be a metaphor, an icon. And though I love snapshots of family and friends, there are times when the camera's reproduction pushes me further away rather than bringing me closer to the people I love most.

But I do have icons. I think we all do, whether we want to admit it or not. I had a very special one for years without realizing that this is what it was. During the almost-decade that we lived in Crosswicks year round, all kinds of things happened to knock my sense of humor out of joint. There were two years when illness or accident kept someone in the hospital so constantly that it became a joke: "Oh, not *you* again!" Friends would telephone, laughing, and ask, "What's happened now?"

Sometime, during those years, I read *The Man in the Grey Flannel Suit*. What I remember from it is the reference to "the tired thirties." I was always tired. So was Hugh. During the decade between thirty and forty, most couples are raising small children, and we were no exception. Hugh was struggling to support his growing family in the strange world outside the theatre. And there was I, absolutely stuck in bucology, with the washing machine freezing at least once a week, the kitchen never above 55° when the wind blew from the northwest, not able to write until after my little ones were in bed, by which time I was so tired that I often quite literally fell asleep with my head on the typewriter.

The various pressures of twentieth-century living have made it almost impossible for the young mother with pre-school children to have any solitude. During the long drag of years before our youngest child went to school, my love for my family and my need to write were in acute conflict. The problem was really that I put two things first. My husband and children came first. So did my writing. Bump.

Crosswicks is isolated, which is one of the things we love about it, but it meant that if the children were to have playmates outside their own siblings, I had to drive them somewhere, or pick up some other children and bring them here. The house was usually full of kids, and that's the way we wanted it, but there were times when for at least a full minute I thought of following Gauguin: I needed a desert island, and time to write.

Well, somehow or other, like a lot of other women who have quite deliberately and happily chosen to be mothers, and work at another vocation as well, I did manage to get a lot of writing done. But during that decade when I was in my thirties, I couldn't sell anything. If a writer says he doesn't care whether he is published or not, I don't believe him. I care. Undoubtedly I care too much. But we do not write for ourselves alone. I write about what concerns me, and I want to share my concerns. I want what I write to be read. Every rejection slip—and you could paper walls with my rejection slips—was like the rejection of me, myself, and certainly of my *amour-propre*. I learned all kinds of essential lessons during those years of rejection, and I'm glad to have had them, but I wouldn't want to have to go through them again. (I'm getting to icons: wait.)

I was, perhaps, out of joint with time. Two of my books for children were rejected for reasons which would be considered absurd today. Publisher after publisher turned down *Meet the Austins* because it begins with a death. Publisher after publisher turned down *A Wrinkle in Time* because it deals overtly with the problem of evil, and it was too difficult for children, and was it a children's or an adults' book, anyhow? My adult novels were rejected, too. *A Winter's Love* was *too* moral: the married protagonist refuses an affair because of the strength of her responsibility towards marriage. Then, shortly before my fortieth birthday, both *Meet the Austins* and an adult novel, *The Lost Innocent*, had been in publishing houses long enough to get my hopes up. I knew that *The Lost Innocent* was being considered very seriously; one editor was strong for it; another was almost equally enthusiastic; a third hated it; and they were waiting for the opinion of a fourth editor who had just come back from Europe. I tried not to think about it, but this was not quite possible. And there was that fortieth birthday coming up.

I didn't dread being forty; I looked forward to it. My thirties had been such a rough decade in so many ways that I was eager for change. Surely, with the new decade, luck would turn.

On my birthday I was, as usual, out in the Tower working on a book. The children were in school. My husband was at work and would be getting the mail. He called, saying, "I'm sorry to have to tell you this on your birthday, but you'd never trust me again if I kept it from you. ———has rejected *The Lost Innocent.*"

This seemed an obvious sign from heaven. I should stop trying to write. All during the decade of my thirties (the world's fifties) I went through spasms of guilt because I spent so much time writing, because I wasn't like a good New England housewife and mother. When I scrubbed the kitchen floor, the family cheered. I couldn't make decent pie crust. I always managed to get something red in with the white laundry in the washing machine, so that everybody wore streaky pink underwear. And with all the hours I spent writing, I was still not pulling my own weight financially.

So the rejection on the fortieth birthday seemed an unmistakable command: Stop this foolishness and learn to make cherry pie.

I covered the typewriter in a great gesture of renunciation. Then I walked around and around the room, bawling my head off. I was totally, unutterably miserable.

Suddenly I stopped, because I realized what my subconscious mind was doing while I was sobbing: my subconscious mind was busy working out a novel about failure.

I uncovered the typewriter. In my journal I recorded this moment of decision, for that's what it was. I had to write. I had no choice in the matter. It was not up to me to say I would stop, because I could not. It didn't matter how small or inadequate my talent. If I never had another book published, and it was very clear to me that this was a real possibility, I still had to go on writing.

I'm glad I made this decision in the moment of failure. It's easy to say you're a writer when things are going well. When the decision is made in the abyss, then it is quite clear that it is not one's own decision at all.

In the moment of failure I knew that the idea of Madeleine, who had to write in order to be, was not image.

And what about that icon?

During those difficult years I was very much aware that if I lost my ability to laugh, I wouldn't be able to write, either. If I started taking myself and my failure too seriously, then the writing would become something that was *mine*, that I could manipulate, that I could take personal credit—or discredit—for. When a book was rejected, I would allow myself twenty-four hours of private unhappiness. I'm sure I wasn't as successful in keeping my misery from the family as I tried to be, but I did try. Our house fronts on a dirt road—we didn't have the land with the brook, then—and I would go down the lane to do my weeping. I found that I could play games with the children during dinner (Buzz and Botticelli were our favorites), but I couldn't listen to Bach. But perhaps what was most helpful—and still is—is a white china laughing Buddha which sits on my desk in the Tower. He laughs at me, never with ridicule, but lovingly, tolerantly: you *are* taking yourself seriously, aren't you, Madeleine? What matters is the book itself. If it is as good a book as you can write at this moment in time, that is what counts. Success is pleasant; of course you want it; but it isn't what makes you write.

No, it's not. I found that out on the morning of my fortieth birthday.

My white china Buddha is an icon. He has never become an idol.

.. 6 ..

My fiftieth birthday was quite unlike my fortieth, but equally memorable, and lots funnier. I always remind people about my birthdays; nobody is ever able to say, "But why didn't you tell me?" I start telling weeks ahead. A birthday, mine, my family's, my friends', is an opportunity for a feast day, a party, for getting together. When it came time for my fiftieth birthday I thought to myself: Half a century! This time I don't need to remind anybody. They'll surely do something splendid.

So I was silent.

The twenty-ninth of November that year was the day after Thanksgiving. Josephine and Alan had gone to England at the end of the summer. Maria was home, and had brought her current beau. Hugh was in previews for a play which was to open the following week, so he was legitimately preoccupied. Tom Tallis was coming for my birthday dinner, and he had also procured, through an Iranian friend, a real, right, and proper hookah for Bion, who is one of his innumerable godchildren— only he knows how many: I think he said that our granddaughter Charlotte is the twenty-ninth.

On that fiftieth, half-century, birthday, it was obvious that, under all the circumstances, I would have to cook dinner, rather than be taken out. So I cooked it, an excellent dinner, roast beef, red and juicy; broccoli with hollandaise sauce; Yorkshire pudding; all the assorted accompanying goodies. Tallis had brought some splendid champagne. We had barely finished dinner when Hugh had to rush off to the theatre. Maria and her friend had a party to go to; Bion and Tallis played with the hookah and drank up all my champagne; and I did the dishes. While I was getting things organized in the kitchen, the two dogs, Oliver and Tyrrell, stole the rest of the roast beef from the sideboard and ate it.

Alan wrote me from England, "Madeleine, you were so good about not reminding people about your birthday this year."

I wrote back, "Never again. My birthday is the twenty-ninth of November and next year I will be fifty-one and I want people to DO something about it."

The fortieth. The fiftieth. And the sixtieth? It's still almost a decade off. It's not up to me to think about it. Or where I may be.

.. 7 ..

The title of a book is as important as one's right and proper signature on a check. A book may have a Library of Congress number, as a check may have that cybernetic salad, but a book, like Emily Brontë, like you, like me, must have its own name. Some books get born with names: *The Arm of the Starfish. The Young Unicorns.* We had to search for the proper name for *A Wrinkle in Time,* and it was my mother who came up with it, during a night of insomnia. I went into her room with a cup of coffee in the morning, and she said, "I think I have a title for your book, and it's right out of the text: A Wrinkle in Time." Of course! It's perfect.

But what to call this book? It's gone through a number of names, some proposed by me, some by friends. The final title was brought up by Bob Giroux, right out of the text. But before he came on it, there were several other names which we considered. *The Burning Bush*. Not bad. In a sense it's what the book is about. But it sounds too philosophical, and as though I were about to come up with answers to unanswerable questions. No; it's out.

The full first draft of the book was written during a Crosswicks summer. Crosswicks means *where the two roads meet*. What about that as a title? Hugh and I rather liked it. F S & G didn't.

Then Hugh suggested, also out of the text, *On the One Hand*. That, too, was vetoed.

Tallis, sitting in the Crosswicks living room, resplendent in his kilt, proposed *Word, Words, and the Word*. Yes, that's a fine title, but it seems too big, too grand, for this book which is essentially small and personal: a letter.

My *Letter from Crosswicks*. (That's how I think of it.)

A letter to the world? In a sense, yes. But that's still too big, too general. And this, like all letters, is particular.

To whom, then, is it addressed?

It is first and foremost a letter to Hugh, my husband who has put up with me for almost twenty-five years. And then it's a letter to all the librarians, teachers, students, who have been so warm and generous and giving with me during these past few years as I've traveled about the country on speaking and teaching jaunts. And it's to Clare Costello and Liz Nichols and Martha King, who asked me to write it, Clare and Liz several years ago; Martha, just this past July at O.S.U. To them all I replied, brushing it off, "It's a lovely idea, but not for me. I'm a storyteller. I have a hard enough time writing a twenty-minute lecture, much less a whole book of non-fiction."

But I hadn't been home from O.S.U. for more than a few days when the book woke me up in the middle of the night, clamoring to be written. As usual, I had no choice.

And it is also a letter of love to my mother and my children and the friends of my right hand, like Tallis, those who have made me know who I am, who have taught me the meaning of ontology, who, like my husband, bear with me, pick me up when I fall down, literally and figuratively, for I frequently do both; who shove me back into a sense of proportion and a sense of humor.

My dears: here: to you.

.. 8 ..

Once, when I was very unhappy, Hugh and I had to go to a large cocktail party. There was nothing I wanted to do less than get dressed up and have to radiate charm to swarms of people. But we went, and I tried. There was a woman at the party who very quickly had too much to drink because she was lost; she had been widowed; she had not been able to find a new life which was valuable, or in which she felt she had any value. She talked to me and cried into her drink and suddenly she said, "You're a very happy person, aren't you?"

I had, at that point, legitimate reason to be miserable. But her question stopped me in my tracks. I looked at her in surprise and gratitude and said, "Yes. I am."

This was ten years ago. But the answer is still the same. The better word, of course, is joy, because it doesn't have anything to do with pain, physical or spiritual. I have been wholly in joy when I have been in pain—childbirth is the obvious example. Joy is what has made the pain bearable and, in the end, creative rather than destructive.

To be fifty-one in the world of today and to be able to say, "I am a happy person," may seem irresponsible. But it is not. It is what keeps me capable of making a response. I do not understand it, or need to.

Meanwhile, I am grateful.

And the unknown woman who gave me the revelation is one of the people to whom I am writing this letter.

. . 9 . .

Like all love letters, it is personal; there isn't any other way for me to write it. Just as I realized, that first morning at O.S.U. that I was standing in front of a group of people all of whom were experts in the field in which I was supposed to lecture to them, and my only hope was not to try to be an expert but to offer them myself and all that writing has taught me in the past half century, so my only hope in this book is to do the same thing.

In thinking about my reservations I fall over a kind of false humility which is really only pride. My job is to write the book. That is all. Nothing else.

But pride comes in. Tallis asked me, about a book I had just finished, "How is it?" "I don't know. I never know." I never do know. He pushed me, "But what do you really think of it?" "I think it's good." And this was true, too. If something deep within even the most tentative and minor of artists didn't think his work was good, he would stop, forever.

H. A. Williams (and what an extraordinary world this is: we met and became friends long after I had copied down these words which he wrote while he was at Trinity College in Cambridge) says: "Because the Holy Spirit is within us, because He can be known only subjectively, only, that is, by means of what I am, we shall never feel absolutely certain that it is in fact the

27

Spirit who is working. This is the price that has to be paid for inspiration of every kind. Is it all nonsense after all? I suppose that's why an artist or writer is so sensitive about the reception of his work. If the critics tear it to pieces, they echo his own inevitable doubts of his validity." Yes.

My husband is my most ruthless critic. Tallis runs him a close second. Sometimes he will say, "It's been said better before." Of course. It's all been said better before. If I thought I had to say it better than anybody else, I'd never start. Better or worse is immaterial. The thing is that it has to be said; by me; ontologically. We each have to say it, to say it our own way. Not of our own *will*, but as it comes out through us. Good or bad, great or little: that isn't what human creation is about. It is that we have to try; to put it down in pigment, or words, or musical notations, or we die.

While I was at Smith, Mary Ellen Chase gave a morning talk to the entire college in John M. Greene Hall. What I remember of this particular talk is that she said that literature could be divided into three categories: "Majah, minah, and mediocah." Majah, minah, and mediocah became passwords on campus. I'm sure that all of us who were young and arrogant could not bear the idea that we would ever be either minah or mediocah. When I am thinking straight I know that it is not important. I don't always think straight. There is still in me the childish child who wants to "show" all the teachers, editors, good housewives, or the socially graceful, that I can—as the jargon goes—compete.

Yesterday while I was down by the brook I read the following lines from the fourth chapter of Ecclesiasticus, or the Book of Wisdom, and it could not have been better timed, because I had been feeling deprecatory about my words; I had, in a sense, already been protecting myself against any rejection later on, protecting myself by that destructive false humility. These words took me by the scruff of the neck and threw me back into better perspective:

> . . . do not be over-modest in your own cause,
> for there is a modesty that leads to sin,
> as well as a modesty that brings honour and favour.
> Do not be untrue to yourself in deference to another,
> or so diffident that you fail in your duty . . .
> for wisdom shows itself by speech
> and a man's education must find expression in words. . . .
> Do not let yourself be a doormat to a fool
> or curry favour with the powerful.
> Fight to the death for truth,
> and the Lord God will fight on your side.

Majah, minah, mediocah: it is not my problem.

. . 10 . .

But what about that self-image?

We talked, this July in Columbus, about how you can be walking down the street and you will catch a glimpse of yourself reflected in a store window and think: who is that? Oh, no, it's not!

But it is.

We really don't know what we look like. We are moderately careful to spend a certain amount of time in front of the mirror; we choose the mirror before which we comb our hair, shave, or put on lipstick or eyeshadow, with a good deal of attention. We don't use a distorted mirror, or ones like those in the fun houses at fairs and carnivals. The bathroom mirror tells us a certain amount about our outside selves.

But the inner, essential self?

I don't know what I'm like. I get glimpses of myself in other people's eyes. I try to be careful whom I use as a mirror: my husband; my children; my mother; the friends of my right hand. If I do something which disappoints them I can easily read it in their response. They mirror their pleasure or approval, too.

But we aren't always careful of our mirrors. I'm not. I made the mistake of thinking that I "ought" not to write because I wasn't making money, and therefore in the eyes of many people around me I had no business to spend hours every day at the typewriter. I felt a failure not only because my books weren't being published but because I couldn't emulate our neighboring New England housewives. I was looking in the wrong mirrors. I still do, and far too often. I catch myself at it, but usually afterwards. If I have not consciously thought, "What will the neighbors think?" I've acted as though I had.

I've looked for an image in someone else's mirror, and so have avoided seeing myself.

We did manage, that morning in Columbus, to delete the word *image*. "All right," Yetta said, "I think I understand. But I still think we need to give the child a self."

But when I was getting ready for bed that night it occurred to me that no teacher can hope to give the child a self unless the teacher knows what a self is, unless the teacher *is* a self. Here we are, living in a world of "identity crises," and most of us have no idea what an identity is.

Half the problem is that an identity is something which must be understood intuitively, rather than in terms of provable fact. An infinite question is often destroyed by finite answers. To define everything is to annihilate much that gives us laughter and joy. I found that I could think about this strange thing, the self, only in terms of the characters in the novel I was writing, or in terms of other people, never of myself. If I try self-consciously to become a person, I will never be one. The most real people, those who are able to forget their selfish selves, who have true compassion, are usually the most distinct individuals. But that comes second. Personhood comes first, and our civilization tempts, if not teaches, us to reverse the process.

As usual, we bump into paradox and contradiction.

The people I know who are the most concerned about their individuality, who probe constantly into motives, who are always turned inwards towards their own reactions, usually become less and less individual, less and less spontaneous, more and more afraid of the consequences of giving themselves away. They are perhaps more consistent than the rest of us, but also less real.

When Alan first started reading his thesis to me, he was concerned that Herbert Kelly, about whom he was writing, came out as a contradictory character. But Kelly *was* contradictory, and I said, "Why shouldn't he be? The deeper and richer a personality is, the more full it is of paradox and contradiction. It's only a shallow character who offers us no problems of contrast." A perfect person would be inhuman. I like the fact that in ancient Chinese art the great painters always included a deliberate flaw in their work: human creation is never perfect.

We find the same thing in literature. The truly great books are flawed: *The Brothers Karamazov* is unwieldy in structure; a present-day editor would probably want to cut the Grand Inquisitor scene because it isn't necessary to the plot. For me, *The Brothers Karamazov* is one of the greatest novels ever written, and this is perhaps because of, rather than in spite of, its human faults. *Hamlet* is usually considered Shakespeare's finest play, and yet nobody has ever satisfactorily, once and for all, been able to analyze or pin down Hamlet's character.

When I start a new seminar I tell my students that I will undoubtedly contradict myself, and that I will mean both things. But an acceptance of contradiction is no excuse for fuzzy thinking. We do have to use our minds as far as they will take us, yet acknowledging that they cannot take us all the way.

We *can* give a child a self-image. But is this a good idea? Hitler did a devastating job at that kind of thing. So does Chairman Mao. To settle for this because we can't give a child a self is manipulation, coercion, and ultimately the coward's way out.

I haven't defined a self, nor do I want to. A self is not something static, tied up in a pretty parcel and handed to the child, finished and complete. A self is always becoming. *Being* does mean becoming, but we run so fast that it is only when we seem to stop—as sitting on the rock at the brook—that we are aware of our own *isness*, of being. But certainly this is not static, for this awareness of being is always a way of moving from the selfish self—the self-image—and towards the real.

Who am I, then? Who are you?

.. 11 ..

I first became aware of myself as self, as Pascal's reed ("Man is only a reed, the feeblest reed in nature; but he is a thinking reed"), when I was seven or eight years old. We lived in an apartment on East 82nd Street in New York. My bedroom window looked out on the court, and I could see into the apartments across the way. One evening when I was looking out I saw a woman undressing by her open window. She took off her dress, stretched, stood there in her slip, not moving, not doing anything, just standing there, being.

And that was my moment of awareness (of ontology?): that woman across the court who did not know me, and whom I did not know, was a person. She had thoughts of her own. She *was*. Our lives would never touch. I would never know her name. And yet it was she who revealed to me my first glimpse of personhood.

When I woke up in the morning the wonder of that revelation was still with me. There was a woman across the court, and she had dreams and inner conversations which were just as real as mine and which did not include me. But she was there, she was real, and so, therefore, was everybody else in the world. And so, therefore, was I.

I got out of bed and stood in front of the mirror and for the first time looked at myself consciously. I, too, was real, standing there thin and gawky in a white nightgown. I did more than exist. I *was*.

That afternoon when I went to the park I looked at everybody I passed on the street, full of the wonder of their realness.

. . 12 . .

I could share this experience with my friends in Ohio, although I still could not tell them how to give a child a self, or what a self is. And I had another experience to share with them, one which helps me to get a glimpse of the burning bush out of the corner of my eye.

We hadn't spent more than one winter at Crosswicks when I found myself the choir director in the village church. I had no

33

qualifications as choir director beyond a passionate love of music, and I knew nothing about church music; in fact, since the crisis in faith (more jargon) that so often comes during college, I had seldom darkened the doors of a church when a service was going on. Neither had my husband.

But when our children were born, two things happened simultaneously. We cleaned up our language; we had been careless about four-letter words—I'd been rather proud of those I'd picked up from stage hands; we no longer used them indiscriminately. And we discovered that we did not want our children to grow up in a world which was centered on man to the exclusion of God. We did know that bedtime prayers were not enough and that it made no sense whatsoever to send the children to Sunday School unless we went to church ourselves. The inconsistency of parents who use the church as a free baby-sitting service on Sunday mornings, while they stay home and read the Sunday papers, did not have to be pointed out to us. I found myself earnestly explaining to the young minister that I did not believe in God, "but I've discovered that I can't live as though I didn't believe in him. As long as I don't need to say any more than that I try to live as though I believe in God, I would very much like to come to church—if you'll let me."

So I became the choir director. Grandma was the organist and she had been the organist since she started playing for Sunday School when she was eleven years old, and she was, when we first knew her, up in her eighties. She had had a large family, and in all those years had missed only two Sundays. Hugh and I visualized Grandma rushing through the last hymn just in time to go have her baby so she could be back in church the following Sunday.

Grandma and I loved each other. She had been distressed

because the church had been for so long without a choir, and would bring in occasional soloists. But the standard of music was low, what I called "Blood of the lamb-y." When I was asked to get together a group of people in the village who might like to sing on a few Sundays during the year, I replied, "No, but I'll start a choir, if you like. And we'll sing every Sunday. Summer, too. God doesn't take the summer off, and if we have a choir, neither will we." I might not believe in God, but I knew that much about him.

The choir was completely volunteer, and completely ecumenical. Before ecumenism was "in," we had Episcopalian, Lutheran, Presbyterian, Dutch Reform, Methodist, and Southern Baptist choristers, and all in the Congregational Church. Musically, I was certainly Episcopalian. It was the church into which I was born, and my father loved good church music. In New York as a child I was taken to church much as I was taken to the opera.

I wanted the choir to be good. I wanted us to sing good music, and to be a success. Some of the volunteer singers had beautiful voices; one had a great one. Some of them couldn't stay in tune and pulled the whole group down into a flat, sodden mass. One woman stayed in key, all right, but at full volume at all times, and with an unpleasant, nasal whine. If the choir was to be a success, the obvious first thing to do was to ease out some of the problem voices.

I couldn't do it. I don't know why, but something told me that every single person in that choir was more important than the music. 'But the music is going to be terrible,' I wailed to this invisible voice. 'That doesn't matter. That's not the reason for this choir.' I didn't ask what was, but struggled along. The extraordinary, lovely thing was that the music got to be pretty good, far better, I am now convinced, than it would have been if I'd put the music first and the people second. I suppose, long before I'd heard the word, I was being ontological.

I did have subversive means of getting my own way about what music we sang. I'd bring out something I loved, Palestrina, for instance, and everybody would groan, so I'd put it away. A couple of weeks later I'd bring it out again, and someone would remark, "That's kind of nice." "I'm afraid it's too difficult for us," I'd say, and put it away again. Two more weeks, and out it would come, and someone would exclaim, "That's beautiful! Can we learn that?" And we did, and everybody loved it. I, in my turn, learned to love some of the music I had felt "above."

As the choir developed, choice of music became limited by only one factor: Grandma, growing older, could no longer play in sharps. I felt great sympathy with her in this. Flats are lots easier than sharps for me, too. At first she could play in three sharps, then two, and finally none. Quinn, our young minister, would select hymns which fitted well with his sermon, and I'd have to say, "Sorry, Quinn, you can't have that; it's in four sharps."

And Grandma preferred major to minor. But, because we loved each other, that was no problem. I'd put my arm about her tiny, bowed little back (her legs could barely stretch to reach the organ pedals) and say, "Grandma, will you let us sing this, please? I know it's minor, but we've done major anthems for three weeks, and I love this one." "All right, Madeleine. For you." I don't think Grandma ever liked the minor anthems, but she played them most graciously.

Grandma and the choir taught me something about persons, how to be a self myself, and how to honor the self in others.

.. 13 ..

One evening I went to choir rehearsal; in the morning's mail
had been a rejection slip. The choir was singing well, and I
went to the back of the church to listen to the anthem and see if
the voices were balanced, and caught myself thinking bitterly,
"Is this all I'm good for? to direct a second-rate choir in a village
church?"

I was in that area of despair where one is incapable of being
ontological. In my definition of the word, this is sin.

.. 14 ..

A winter ago I was asked by the Children's Book Council to
write a story, and agreed to do so. I was telling Tallis about it,
and said, "I'm really very nervous about this." He looked at me
contemptuously: "You don't think *you*'re going to have anything to do with it, do you?" "No," I retorted, "but I could get in
the way." Mostly, while I was directing the choir, I didn't get in
the way, and I hadn't yet reached the stage of either understanding or being self-conscious about such things. But getting in the
way does bother me whenever I lead a seminar. It bothered me
at O.S.U., and yet I knew that the moment I started worrying
about whether or not I was good enough for the job, I wouldn't
be able to do it.

If I accept the fact that I, ontologically speaking, was born a
writer, was named Madeleine, am an inextricable blend of
writer, wife, mother, then my virtue, or talent, is quite aside
from the point. When I accepted myself as Madeleine on my
fortieth birthday, not a computer's punch-out, or my social-

security number, or the post-office date on the latest rejection slip, it had nothing to do with the degree of my talent. I could, during the long years of failure, console myself with the fact that van Gogh sold precisely one picture while he lived, and that he was considered an impossible painter. I could try to reassure my agent when he was concerned about the damaging effect on me of so much failure; he was afraid it would kill my talent. Can this happen? I don't know, I just don't know.

I think that all artists, regardless of degree of talent, are a painful, paradoxical combination of certainty and uncertainty, of arrogance and humility, constantly in need of reassurance, and yet with a stubborn streak of faith in their validity, no matter what. When I look back on that decade of total failure— it's been a mixture, both before, and since—there was, even on the days of rejection slips, a tiny, stubborn refusal to be completely put down. And I think, too, and possibly most important, that there is a faith simply in the validity of art; when we talk about ourselves as being part of the company of such people as Mozart or van Gogh or Dostoevsky, it has nothing to do with comparisons, or pitting talent against talent; it has everything to do with a way of looking at the universe. My husband said, "But people might think you're putting yourself alongside Dostoevsky." The idea is so impossible that I can only laugh in incredulity. Dostoevsky is a giant; I look up to him; I sit at his feet; perhaps I will be able to learn something from him. But we do face the same direction, no matter how giant his stride, how small mine.

During that dreadful decade I pinned on my workroom wall a cartoon in which a writer, bearing a rejected manuscript, is dejectedly leaving a publisher's office; the caption says, "We're very sorry, Mr. Tolstoy, but we aren't in the market for a war story right now." That cartoon got me through some bad hours. It didn't mean that I was setting myself beside Tolstoy.

On the other hand I was anything but comforted when Hugh thought to console me by pointing out some published stories which "aren't nearly as good as yours. Doesn't that make you feel better?" "Of course it doesn't make me feel better!" I cried. "You're absolutely right, I write much better than that. Why should it make me feel better to have bad writing published? If it were better than mine, then I wouldn't mind, then I *would* feel better."

It was great writing which kept me going, the company of the Brontës, William Blake, Alexandre Dumas. But there's still pride to fall over, not pride in the sense of self-respect, but in that Greek sense of *hubris*: pride against the gods; do-it-yourself-ism, which the Greeks understood to mean "I can do it myself just as well as, if not better than, the gods." When my hubris gets pricked, I bleed; or at any rate my hubris bleeds. Mine is still sore from something a friend of mine, a friend of the right hand, whom we will call Will, said to me shortly before I went to Ohio: what Will said is that in group conversation I am apt to seem as though I were going to say something extremely important, and then come out with the obvious. I thought of this accusation while I was in Columbus. Certainly much of what I was fumblingly trying to say during the seminars was obvious. But the obvious needs to be said. Sometimes the obvious is so obscured by brilliant analysis that it gets lost.

Am I trying, as I so often do, to rationalize? Do Will's words still rankle—and they do—because the implication was not just that I come out with the obvious, but that my obvious is shallow? But the obvious need not be shallow. Sometimes it is profound and painful, and can be written off only by being called obvious. Not that I think that Will does this—he does not—but it can be a danger for any intellectual.

In another conversation, Will and I discussed the peril of falling into the trap of intellectual elitism. The older I grow, the more this insidious form of snobbery seems a snare and a delusion. We probably have more scientific knowledge at our fingertips today than ever before, and yet we are incapable of handling this knowledge creatively; we cannot avoid mutilating diseases, devastating wars, or control earthquake or tornado; and we are in grave danger of destroying our planet entirely because we cannot control what our intellect has unleashed, from cobalt bombs to polluting laundry detergents.

More personally, my intellect is a stumbling block to much that makes life worth living: laughter; love; a willing acceptance of being created. The rational intellect doesn't have a great deal to do with love, and it doesn't have a great deal to do with art. I am often, in my writing, great leaps ahead of where I am in my thinking, and my thinking has to work its way slowly up to what the "superconscious" has already shown me in a story or poem. Facing this does help to eradicate do-it-yourself hubris from an artist's attitude towards his painting or music or writing. My characters pull me, push me, take me further than I want to go, fling open doors to rooms I don't want to enter, throw me out into interstellar space, and all this long before my mind is ready for it.

There's a reason for that, chaps!

While Alan was in school, his science teacher was an inept young man who kept blowing things up, remarking through the stench of chemical smoke and the crashing of broken glass, "There's a reason for that, chaps."

I must be willing to accept the explosions which take place

deep down in the heart of the volcano, sending up an occasional burst of flame into the daylight of consciousness.

With my naked intellect I cannot believe in God, particularly a loving God. My intellect is convinced that any idea of the person's continuing and growing after death is absurd; logic goes no further than dust to dust. Images, in the literary sense of the word, take me much further. Without my glasses I can see nothing but a vague blur. When I put them on, I become functional. But who is doing the seeing? The lenses of the spectacles are not. I am. There is an essential, ontological me—that part of me which is not consumed in the burning—which is (to use imagery again) that which I was created to be, the imaginative Adam and Eve as they were in the pre-history days of the Garden. Some of our children talk about going back to the garden; we can't do that; but we can travel in the direction which will lead us to that place where we may find out who we really are.

.. 15 ..

Not long ago I was one of several "children's writers" on a panel. I had not been told that we were expected to begin by making a statement as to why we write for children. Because of the seating arrangements, I was "on" second. The first writer had written down his reasons, and good ones they were, too, though not mine. Sometimes when we have to speak suddenly we come closer to the truth than when we have time to think. I said, "I suppose I write for children because I'm not bright enough to understand the difference between a children's and an adults' novel."

These words seem to me to contain considerable truth, as well as considerable naïveté. There's something a little humiliating about having to accept that, at fifty-one, one is naïve. I am. I would, quite often, like to be grownup, wise, and sophisticated. But these gifts are not mine.

I was comforted, two days after the panel, when I read an article on William James, written by a brilliant novelist and essayist, a writer of my own generation, a critic taken seriously by our contemporaries. In this essay it was evident that the author agreed with those who consider James naïve in his attitude towards religion and the supernatural; James's hope for something beyond the abyss of nothingness after death is cited as evidence of his naïveté. With a shock of joy I realized in what good company I am: William James, pushing beyond the rational world to that wilder, freer place on the other side of the intellect. Gregory of Nyssa and his brilliant sister, Macrina, meeting at her deathbed and talking, unashamed and unafraid, of their love for their friends, for each other, and of the extraordinary vistas soon to open for Macrina. Socrates, drinking hemlock, and talking with calm certainty about what lies ahead for him. Many others, all more brilliant, more erudite, more sophisticated than I.

And there are, too, the high-school students who come to me to talk about the transcendent, about God, about the hope for a meaning to all life, no matter how terrible and irrational it may sometimes seem.

I look at many of the brilliant, sophisticated intellectuals of my generation, struggling through psychoanalysis, balancing sleeping pills with waking pills, teetering on the thin edge of despair, and think that perhaps they have not found the answer after all.

Well, of course, neither have I. It is not up to me to do so. I am finite; in the earthly sense, mortal; with a good mind flawed by naïveté; dependent on my friends; on hope; on joy.

.. 16 ..

It is all, as usual, paradox. I have to use what intellect I have in order to write books, but I write the kind of books I do in order that I may try to set down glimpses of things that are on the other side of the intellect. We do not go around, or discard the intellect, but we must go through and beyond it. If we are given minds we are required to use them, but not limit ourselves by them.

It's a strange thing that despite the anti-intellectualism in our country, we also set so much store by I Q's and objective testing in our schools and colleges and businesses. Is passing a course in statistics really a legitimate requirement for a Ph.D.? Does the preliminary testing by which a child is placed in school really tell us enough about him? One of the teachers at O.S.U. brought this up. How do you teach, and show your concern for the student who isn't very bright?

An I Q cannot measure artistic ability. A potential Picasso may be a flop at objective vocabulary or number tests. An I Q does not measure a capacity for love. One of the most moving and perceptive sets of letters I've ever received came from a class of retarded children who had had *A Wrinkle in Time* read aloud to them. Their teacher apologized for their handwriting and mistakes in spelling and grammar; she needn't have; she obviously loved them and had taught them to express love; maybe that's more important than social studies. Maybe that's what Yetta meant by giving the child a self.

Children have helped to give me a self in their conversations with me and in their letters. There are always the letters which are no more than a class assignment: Write an author. But far more often there are letters remarkable for their depth of understanding, and which move me to the point of tears. And, lest I begin to take personal credit, there is a letter—one of my favorites—from a girl who really poured it on: "Dear Miss L'Engle, you are one of the greatest writers of all time," and so on, fulsome phrase after fulsome phrase. She signed her name and then wrote, "P. S. I have not yet read any of your books, but I am sure they will be good when I do." This helps give me a self, too!

How do we teach a child—our own, or those in a classroom—to have compassion: to allow people to be different; to understand that like is not equal; to experiment; to laugh; to love; to accept the fact that the most important questions a human being can ask do not have—or need—answers.

Cynthia, one of our Crosswicks family this summer, is thirteen. She has wanted to be a nurse ever since she can remember, and she'll make a very fine one. She was completely firm with the babies, and they adored her. When Thomas, the amber cat, had a bladder infection, Cynthia decided it would be good practice for her to give him his medication. It isn't easy to give a large and stubborn cat unpleasant medication, but Cynthia managed, and with no help, either. We had been discussing, down by the brook, how nothing really important in life is in the realm of provable fact. Cynthia is pragmatic; she had her doubts.

"What about love?" I asked her as we were crossing the big meadow on the way home. "Can you prove anything about love?"

She held down an old strand of barbed wire for me. "I guess not."

"What *is* love?"

"A feeling."

"No," I said, "a feeling is something love is *not*." Cynthia didn't like this; neither do I, lots of the time.

"Why not?"

I asked her, "You love your parents, don't you?"

"Yes."

"Aren't there some days when all your feelings about them are bad? When you're furious with them, and all you *feel* is anger, or that they've been unfair?"

"Yes."

"But you still love them, don't you?"

"Yes."

We were silent for a while because we were picking daisies to make daisy wreaths for the babies. Cynthia was much more diligent about it than I was; I was thinking more about our conversation than about daisies, or even the babies.

Love can't be pinned down by a definition, and it certainly can't be proved, any more than anything else important in life can be proved. Love is people, is a person. A friend of ours, Hugh Bishop of Mirfield, says in one of his books: "Love is not an emotion. It is a policy." Those words have often helped me when all my feelings were unlovely. In a summer household as large as ours I often have to act on those words. I am slowly coming to understand with my heart as well as my head that love is not a feeling. It is a person.

It also has a lot to do with compassion, and with creation.

There are educationists (as jargon has it) who think that creativity itself can be taught, and who write learned, and frequently dull, treatises on methods of teaching it. It is rather as though they were trying to eat air, with the usual result. The creative impulse, like love, can be killed, but it cannot be taught. What a teacher or librarian or parent can do, in working with children, is to give the flame enough oxygen so that it can burn. As far as I'm concerned, this providing of oxygen is one of the noblest of all vocations.

But even among those who admit that talent, genius, the creative impulse (or whatever one calls it) can neither be taught nor defined, there seem to be two diametrically opposed theories as to what it is. One is expressed most clearly by a group of psychiatrists, many of whom studied with Freud, who have been successful in helping well-known writers to recover from writer's block, so we cannot afford to take them lightly.

A few years ago I came across a definition of the writer in *The New York Times:* "The writer, like the alcoholic and the homosexual, is an orally regressed psychic masochist, and artistic creation is an alibi." I looked across the Sunday paper to my husband: "Darling, did you know that I am an orally regressed psychic masochist and I write only as an alibi?"

It's perfectly possible that this is true, but it still strikes me as hilarious. (Does orally regressed mean being unable to talk? If so, I was orally regressed as a solitary, overshy only child. But ever since I learned that I *could* talk, it has been practically impossible to shut me up.)

I have been accused by several friends and acquaintances of being anti-intellectual (I can't win), and also of being "against psychiatrists." I don't really think I am. That would be as silly as being "against dentists" or "against barbers." I do think that psychiatry is still a very young science, not unlike surgery when the surgeons were barbers. If you absolutely had to have a leg amputated in the seventeenth century, you went to a barber; you didn't rush to him for a scratch. I've seen psychiatry save and redeem. I've also seen people going year after year to psychiatrists or therapists and growing steadily more self-centered.

Most of us like being the center of the universe; no wonder these people don't want to give up their bi-weekly sessions. I've also seen them regress in their work and deteriorate in personal relationships. But, my friends tell me, that means it's a bad psychiatrist. True, perhaps.

I'm still less than happy about the school of psychiatry which says that all writers—and all is meant, not just an occasional crackpot—all writers are Peeping Toms, in the clinical sense; this is not meant as a poetic image. No writer is capable of love. The impulse to write is only a neurotic symptom of disease. Any time a writer mentions a mountain it is a breast image. These doctors see phallic symbols, anal symbols, oral symbols, in everything. Once Hugh and I were invited to a large cocktail party—I'm not sure why, because all the other guests were psychiatrists. I dressed up and put on high-heeled shoes, because my 6′ 3″ husband likes me in them when we go out. When we arrived everybody was standing around, as one does at a cocktail party, and almost every man there was shorter than I am. And my feet hurt. So I took off my uncomfortable elegant shoes and put them under a chair. During the party almost every doctor there came to me and asked me confidentially, "Why did you take off your shoes?" And did not believe me when I told them. Perhaps I did have some devious sexual motive: fascinating thought.

I'm quite willing to admit that all images in all forms of art have multiple meanings, and one of the meanings is usually a sex meaning. Let's just think about mountains: one of the most beautiful mountain ranges in our country is the Grand Tetons, which means the Great Breasts. Why not? The idea of nature as mother is hardly new, and I think I've made it clear that I'm all for the pleasures of the body. When, as a very young girl, I read that Freud said that the baby at its mother's breast experiences sexual pleasure, and so does the mother, I was naïvely shocked. When I nursed my own babies I knew what he meant; it was pure sensual delight. It was also an unmitigated act of love, an affirmation of creation.

But I think we tend to confuse the word sex, in the sense of rutting, with the enjoyment of our senses. Breasts are to be enjoyed, and to name the Grand Tetons thus is wholly appropriate. Then, when we read, "And it shall come to pass in the last days, that the mountain of the Lord's house shall be established in the top of the mountains, and shall be exalted above the hills," or, "Sometimes we see a cloud that's dragonish; / A Vapour sometime like a bear or lion, / A tower'd citadel, a pendant rock, / A forked mountain, or blue promontory / With trees upon't, that nod unto the world / And mock our eyes with air: thou hast seen these signs; / They are black vesper's pageants," the imagery expands. An image, this kind of image, like the reality it stands for, always touches on mystery.

I'm always a little doubtful about people who complain about the vast sums spent on such things as moon exploration, saying that none of this is necessary for our military defenses. Whether or no, the practical reasons aren't why we want to explore space. We must push out to the moon, the solar system, our galaxy, the galaxies beyond, because they are there, because they are mysterious. We must explore them in the same way that our great-grandparents pushed across the prairies in covered wagons, not knowing what lay beyond the mountains; in much the same way that Abraham left the comfort of home and went out into the wilderness.

As our heads reel with the enormity of the macrocosm without us, we turn and become dizzy with the microcosm within us; the world of the physicist who pursues the infinitely small things in the physical world; and the psychologists who are exploring the depths of our personalities: I am all for this as long as we remember mystery; as long as we don't ignore joy. The people who would limit art to a neurosis totally forget about joy.

I have a friend, a beautiful and talented young woman, who is afraid to have a child and who is afraid to use her talent to write. She does not yet understand the joy that follows the pain of birth. I've experienced the pain and joy of the birth of babies and the birth of books and there's nothing like it: when a child who has been conceived in love is born to a man and woman, the joy of that birth sings throughout the universe. The joy of writing or composing or painting is much the same, and the insemination comes not from the artist himself but from his relationship with those he loves, with the whole world.

All real art is, in its true sense, religious; it is a religious impulse; there is no such thing as a non-religious subject. But much bad or downright sacrilegious art depicts so-called religious subjects. I've had some glorious times visiting the Sisters and lecturing to the novices at Mundelein College. On my first visit, the Sisters, knowing that I was not Roman Catholic but Anglican, were terribly curious about me; never have I had so many questions asked, questions about ultimate things, questions that put me on my toes: I felt like a strange life-form from another planet being questioned by the natives. Early in the day, when we were all still a little tentative with each other, several of the professed nuns were taking me on a tour of the dormitories. In one of the rooms was what I thought to be an appalling picture of Jesus, wishy-washy, powerless, plain bad art. The senior nun fixed me with a stern eye and demanded, "Madeleine, what do you think of that?" I swallowed and answered, "I think it's ghastly." To which the Sisters chorused, "Oh, thank God."

That so-called sacred picture was totally secular. Conversely, much great religious art has been written or painted or composed by people who thought they were atheists. Picasso, for instance, makes me think of Dorothy Sayers's story of the Japanese gentleman who, in discussing the mysterious concept of the Trinity in Christianity, said, "Honorable Father, very good. Honorable Son, very good. Honorable Bird I do not understand at all."

Very few of us understand Honorable Bird, except to acknowledge that without his power and grace nothing would be written, painted, or composed at all. To say anything beyond this about the creative process is like pulling all the petals off a flower in order to analyze it, and ending up having destroyed the flower.

Now I don't suppose I'd react quite so sharply to those petal-pullers, the writers of psychiatric books who call writers of fiction Peeping Toms, if there weren't a grain of truth in what they say. A writer does need to have a tremendous curiosity about everything and everyone, to have a trained and insatiable awareness. But this must go along with an honest commitment to and involvement in human nature, as against the ghoulish curiosity which makes some people gorge themselves on the newspapers that concentrate on bloody accidents, murders, and sex crimes. This kind of curiosity is selfish, and is in the wrong sense detached from the scenes which it is lasciviously compelled to observe.

Detachment and involvement: the artist must have both. The link between them is compassion. It has taken me over fifty years to begin to get a glimmer of what this means.

Several years ago two of my friends in far-flung places, one in Europe, one in the Northwest, both made the mistake of writing to me—the letters arrived within a week of each other—that I was a harp string, constantly vibrating. I don't remember their exact phrasing, but the general idea was that I was sensitive, vulnerable, quivering with pain, my own and everybody else's, and that this came out in my writing, particularly in my poems, some of which I was sharing with them.

The trouble with this lovely metaphorical comparison was that it made me take myself—not my verses, but myself—far too seriously. My vulnerable vanity was definitely tickled by the comparison to the sensitive artist, delicately tuned, suffering more than duller folk . . .

I'm not sure what laughed me out of this, but something did, promptly; it might have been simply walking into the apartment and having my kids call out, "Hey, Mother, what's for dinner?" or, "Don't burn the peas again tonight."

Compassion means to suffer with, but it doesn't mean to get lost in the suffering, so that it becomes exclusively one's own. I tend to do this, to replace the person for whom I am feeling compassion with myself.

I learned this—though it's still a bit of a problem—shortly after Hugh and I were married, and I was pregnant with our first child. I answered the telephone to learn that a friend of ours had lost a child, a twelve-year-old girl who was thrown from a horse and killed. And I was lost, not in compassion but in passion. The child's mother was an old friend of Hugh's; I didn't know her very well; if I had, certainly my own suffering over the death of her child (the death of all children; the death, potentially, of my child) would have made me completely useless to her. I did realize this, dimly, even while thinking that Hugh was being far too objective about it; that he wasn't *feeling* a thing.

I am just learning to realize what Cynthia and I talked about. It is not that in compassion one cuts oneself off from feeling, only from one's own selfishness, self-centeredness.

It's an odd thing, another paradox, this balance of involvement and detachment, and perhaps one should not think about it too self-consciously. But I get asked about it, and so I try to fumble for a partial answer. We cannot afford, either as writers or as human beings, to be detached from the human predicament, because this is what we write about, and it is the predicament we ourselves are in. We are always on stage, actors in the human drama. But we are also and simultaneously members of the audience: it takes both performer and audience to "create" a drama.

This awareness came to my creative unconscious long before I understood it with my mind. One of the first assignments given by Leonard Ehrlich, who came to Smith for a year to teach writing, and who is one of the many teachers to whom I owe an eternal debt of gratitude, was to write a story in the present tense, using the first person. I wrote an oddly detached story, one that I was at that time really incapable of writing. But it wrenched itself out of me, leaving me physically drained and emotionally exhilarated. It was the story of a painter watching his wife die; he loved her; he was in an agony of grief; he hated his friends who did or who did not come to help. But all the time his wife was dying he could not stop one part of his mind from considering exactly how to paint her, how to mix the colors to show the shadow of death moving across her face.

Of course I didn't realize then that the story was teaching me the ambivalence of involvement/detachment, subjectivity/objectivity that happens to all artists. I say "happens" advisedly; we cannot make ourselves detached; this would be slightly demonic. But we can try, when we write, to be objective. Shortly after writing this story I read Chekhov's letters and copied in my journal: "When you depict sad or unhappy people, and want to touch people's hearts, try to be colder—it gives their grief a background against which it stands out in sharper relief." And he went on to say that the writer does—and must—suffer with his characters, but he "must do this so that the reader does not notice it. The more objective, the stronger will be the effect."

An English poet—I copied his uncredited words in my journal over twenty years ago—said that poetry is like ice cream; tremendous heat is needed in generating it, but during the actual "making" there must be ice, otherwise the ice cream will melt. All the scenes that move me deeply while I am writing them end up in the wastepaper basket.

Kierkegaard says, "A poet is an unhappy creature whose heart is tortured by deepest suffering but whose lips are so formed that when his sighs and cries stream out over them, their sound becomes like the sound of beautiful music. . . . And men flock about the poet saying, 'Sing for us soon again; that is to say, may new sufferings torture your soul, and may your lips continue to be formed as before.' "

All right, but I'd better not take it too seriously; at any rate, I'd better not *feel* it. If I become subjective about pain, no matter what causes it, then it becomes destructive, not creative. Colette said to a young poet who complained to her that he was unhappy, "Mais personne ne t'a demandé d'être heureux. Travaille!"

. . 17 . .

Is the impulse to write, to work out one's unhappiness in work, neurotic? I couldn't care less. In one of her books, Dr. Karen

Horney describes the neurotic personality, detailing the symptoms, and remarks: At this point probably every one of you is going to think, I have all these symptoms. The difference is that the neurotic personality is controlled *by* the symptoms, and the healthy personality is in control of them.

A young priest friend said to me one day at lunch that he is disturbed by his brethren giving so much importance to the "mental health" of themselves and their flocks. "It is a very bad thing," he said, "when we confuse mental health and sanctity."

That night during a wakeful period I thought about all the people in history, literature, art, whom I most admire: Mozart, Shakespeare, Homer, El Greco, St. John, Chekhov, Gregory of Nyssa, Dostoevsky, Emily Brontë: not one of them would qualify for a mental-health certificate. It's been a small game with me this summer to ask, "Do *you* know anybody you really admire, who has really been important to the world in a creative way, who would qualify for a mental-health certificate?" So far nobody has come up with one.

What is mental health, anyhow? If we were all what is generally thought of as mentally healthy, I have a terrible fear that we'd all be alike. Even as we're rushing towards the end of another thousand years, we are still terrified by nonconformity; our nonconforming hippies are at least as conformist as the conformists against whom they are rebelling. I can't think of one great human being in the arts, or in history generally, who conformed, who succeeded, as educational experts tell us children must succeed, with his peer group. We discussed this at Ohio State, and it worried the young teachers. If a child in their classrooms does not succeed with his peer group, then it would seem to many that both child and teacher have failed.

Have they? If we ever, God forbid, manage to make each child succeed with his peer group, we will produce a race of bland and faceless nonentities, and all poetry and mystery will vanish from the face of the earth. Somehow I am not too worried. Surely every teacher must want each child to succeed, with Yetta must hope to help him find a self, but this self may be a nonconforming self. And surely there will always be the occasional prickly child who rejects all efforts, who kicks the other children, bites teacher's hand, is unloving and unlovable, and yet who will, one day, produce—perhaps out of this very unloveliness—a work of art which sings of love.

I am encouraged as I look at some of those who have listened to their "different drum": Einstein was hopeless at school math and commented wryly on his inadequacy in human relations. Winston Churchill was an abysmal failure in his early school years. Byron, that revolutionary student, had to compensate for a club foot; Demosthenes for a stutter; and Homer was blind. Socrates couldn't manage his wife, and infuriated his countrymen. And what about Jesus, if we need an ultimate example of failure with one's peers?

Or an ultimate example of love?

.. 18 ..

I've known for a long time that we know nothing about love, that we do not have love, until we give it away. Grandma showed me this very clearly during my choir-directing days.

In a sense Grandma was the organ, and the organ was Grandma; it was, as McLuhan might say, an extension of Grandma. She lived alone with Grandpa in a tiny little house, and if Grandpa was her love, the organ was her vocation, and one cannot have a vocation without love. Grandpa was old, even older than Grandma, and not well; often she would be up with him all night. It wasn't a surprise to anybody when one morning Grandpa simply did not wake up.

Two days earlier one of Grandma's cousins and close friends had died, and she was to be buried the afternoon of the day that Grandpa died. People asked, "But who will play the organ for the funeral?"

Her daughter called me. "Madeleine, Grandma wants to play for Grandpa's funeral. What shall we do?"

My response was, "You can't take the organ away from Grandma, today of all days. Let her do whatever she wants to do."

Grandma played, of course. To keep everybody happy (she loved us all that much), she got a friend in to play an anthem. But she herself sat at the organ for the rest of the service.

I'm not sure how long after this it was that a man and his wife started some vicious and absurdly untrue gossip about Hugh and me and three other couples, all with jobs in the church: we were, between us, a trustee, a deacon, Sunday School superintendent, Sunday School teachers, choir members and director, and general scrubbers. The man and his wife were leaving town, and why they wanted to destroy those of us who had tried to be their friends we will never know. They were, I suppose, sick (the wife was what my godmother once called menopoisonous), and their lies were so fantastic that one could only be amazed, not angry. Basically, the accusation was that we were all Communist agents. It would have been funny indeed except for one thing: people were eager to believe the lies. It was during the sad reign of Senator Joseph McCarthy; witch-hunting was in the air; but we were still unprepared.

We ought not to have been so shocked and hurt. An eagerness to believe ill of others in order to feel virtuous oneself is to some extent in all of us. It is perhaps more visible in small communities. Certainly it is not unique in our village. But we *were* hurt, desperately hurt. Hugh and I knew nothing about it until Thanksgiving afternoon, when the other three couples asked if they could come over for a conference. At first it seemed so incredible that we tended not to take it seriously, to laugh, and probably that was what we ought to have done. But our laughter stopped. Someone said, "If that's the way they feel about us, if they want us out of the church, then I think we ought to get out. I think the thing to do is for all of us to resign. I don't mean that we should stop going to church, but we shouldn't hold any offices in it."

This was the consensus. I was the lone voice saying, "No!" I loved the choir; I loved my high-school Sunday free-for-all discussion group; I might be terribly unsure about God, but I was happy working in his house. I said, "If we resign, it's admitting that they're right about us." But finally I gave in, so that the resignation would be unanimous. We wrote it out—I forget exactly what we said—and sent it to the senior and junior deacons.

In a village our size, everybody knows everybody: the senior deacon was the father of two of the brightest boys in my discussion group; the junior deacon, who would become senior deacon at the first of the year, is our family doctor; his youngest daughter was—still is—one of our daughter Josephine's friends. This kind of close relationship existed for all of us.

So we waited for their response.

And went to choir rehearsal.

The story, in various versions, was, of course, all over town. When I walked into the church Grandma was there to meet me; she had to talk to me before we started rehearsal. Now, I was quite certain that Grandma would have heard the whole sorry tale from a great many people who would like to see us put down. I loved Grandma, and I thought that Grandma loved me, but I doubted her.

Grandma said to me, "Madeleine, I just want you to know that if you go, I go, too."

Grandma was offering to give up the organ. Grandma was giving me herself.

That absolute gesture of love is what remains with me.

The deacons tore up our resignation. The gossip blew over—though, after all these years, there are still a few people with whom I feel very tentative. But only a few.

. . 19 . .

Grandma gave me herself, and so helped to give me myself. Is that what Yetta was getting at? Yetta being Yetta, I think it was. But it's one thing to talk consciously about giving oneself away and another to do it, for it must be done completely unselfconsciously; it is not a do-it-yourself activity. No computer can teach it; no computer can show a child compassion, or how to allow people to be different, to experiment, to love. Almost all the joyful things of life are outside the measure of I Q tests, are beyond the realm of provable fact. A person is needed. But if any teacher, no matter how qualified, no matter how loving, goes into a classroom thinking, "I am going to give a child a self," it can't possibly happen.

Zeke, one of the Fellows at O.S.U., saw this quickly. Zeke is a Ph.D. candidate, father of four, lay preacher in a Pentecostal church; we couldn't come from more different traditions, but we found that we had all the essential things in common. The morning after Yetta had started the discussion on giving the child a self, Zeke brought me this quotation from G. A. Young, an Omaha psychiatrist: "The compulsion for me to get my cotton-pickin' fingers on my fellow man is the natural result of my belief that I have the *word*. If I do have the word and feel surrounded by unmolded clay, I have no choice but to mold. When I do this, I begin playing God, and as a result usually raise the devil."

"Oh, yes," I said, "let's share this with everybody." And I had a similar quotation for Zeke, written about a hundred years earlier, by George MacDonald, Congregational parson and writer of superb fantasy for both children and adults. I had taken with me to Ohio a small collection of extracts from Mac-Donald, compiled by C. S. Lewis, and read the following quotation one morning before breakfast, and wrote in my journal that it was vitally important for me to remember it during the two Writer in Residence weeks: "Am I going to do a good deed? Then, of all times,—Father, into thy hands: lest the enemy should have me now."

Just as I had wanted to copy the G. A. Young, Zeke wanted to copy the MacDonald.

"There's one sort of important difference," I said, tentatively, because it was just coming into my conscious mind, and I wasn't sure I could find the right words for it. "George Mac-Donald implies that as long as we put ourselves into God's hands, then maybe something good *can* happen, not because of us, but because he helps. I have a feeling that if I read only G. A. Young, I'd be terrified ever to enter a classroom again, or start another book." And then I said, "I've just remembered another quotation: this one's from the Psalms. Whenever I'm going to teach a class or give a speech, I always think of it, and hold onto it: Not unto us, O Lord, not unto us, but unto thy Name give the praise; for thy loving mercy, and for thy truth's sake."

"Yes," Zeke said, and marked that down, too.

It was easy to say this to Zeke, because we work from the same premise. It wasn't easy to say it to the entire group. I'm always afraid of sounding pompous, or pious, in the pejorative sense of piosity. When I was an extremely naughty child in an English boarding school, the worst thing that we could call anybody was "pi." I still think it's an abominable characteristic.

And, I suppose, quoting MacDonald and the Psalms, and then sounding off about them myself, I was afraid of looking as though I were going to deliver a mountain and coming forth with a mouse: of being obvious.

I wonder if I will ever learn not to apologize for the obvious?

.. 20 ..

There has been much to teach me about the ontology of things this summer: the blueberry bush; Thomas, the amber cat, and Tyrrell, the large amber dog, diligently washing each other's faces in harmony and amity; the younger members of the Crosswicks family climbing up onto our big four-poster bed for hot chocolate at midnight; the babies' incredibly beautiful bare bodies as I help give them their baths before dinner: all these, and many more awarenesses, are proof of my word for this summer.

It is this kind of awareness which I demand from my students in the seminar in writing practices I give somewhere or other each year. I like the name *writing practices* better than *Creative Writing*. As I have said, nobody can teach creative writing—run like mad from anybody who thinks he can. But one can teach practices, like finger exercises on the piano; one can share the tools of the trade, and what one has gleaned from the great writers: it is the great writers themselves who do the teaching, rather than the leader of a seminar. It doesn't take long for the gifted student to realize that there are certain things the great writers always do, and certain things they never do; it is from these that we learn.

Henry James tells us: *Render, do not report.* The writing of fiction is an entirely different discipline from the writing of journalism, and I have to warn my students that I can teach them nothing about journalism; a journalist *must* report; he tells, rather than shows. The two techniques are almost diametrically opposite. The writer of fiction—and I include in this all the works of the imagination, poetry, plays, realistic novels, fantasy—may never tell; he must show, and show through the five senses. "Describe this room in which we're sitting," I say, "and make use of all five of your senses. Don't tell us. Show us." The beginning writer finds this difficult. I have to repeat and repeat: fiction is built upon the concrete. A news article is essentially transitory and may be built upon sand. The house of fiction must be built upon rock. Feel, smell, taste, hear, see: *show* it.

Dante says: "You cannot understand what I write unless you understand it in a fourfold way: on the literal level, the moral level, the allegorical level, and the anagogical level." What is this anagogical level? It's not easy to define, because it is out of the realm of provable fact. It is most easily discernible in the great works of fantasy, such as Dante's own *Inferno.* The best science fiction is anagogical; the Apocalypse is anagogical. Thinking about icons helps me to understand what Dante meant by the word "anagogical." I do not believe that it is a level that is ever used consciously even by the greatest writers. It is that level of a book which breaks the bounds of time and space and gives us a glimpse of the truth, that truth which casts the shadows into Plato's cave, the shadows which are all we mortals are able to see.

I have had to accept that one cannot talk even in the most technical way about the writing of fiction, without talking about being (the why of the blueberry bush). Even the driest rules of syntax involve, in their explication, a sharing of self. Someone asks, for instance, why we need bother with syntax at all. I reply that Herbert Read says that the only difference between man and beast is syntax; and a hot discussion is on. I would worry more about our digressions if some very fine writing didn't come out of these seminars.

All explanations involve particulars; one cannot render without being specific. Try to explain anything in generalities: it just doesn't work. There are particular rules to the baking of a cake (I can hear my family and friends asking: "How would *you* know? when did you last bake a cake?" I'll tell you about my last cake later; it's important), the cooking of a boeuf bourguignon (I do know how to do that), or the putting together of an automobile engine, or a radio, or a television set. This need for particularity is equally true in storytelling. The great writers start out by giving the reader, immediately, the ontology of the protagonist; or, to put it in the form of a literary rule, a writer should immediately tell the reader four things:

1: Who the story is about.
2: What he is doing.
3: Where he is doing it.
4: When he is doing it.

The reader must be placed in action, space, and time. In a good story we find out very quickly about the hero the things we want to know about ourselves.

One cannot discuss structure in writing without discussing

structure in all life; it is impossible to talk about why anybody writes a book or paints a picture or composes a symphony without talking about the nature of the universe. I warn my students that when I get dogmatic about such weighty matters it is usually when I am most unsure of myself. "Any time I make a categorical statement, and I'm going to make lots of them during these sessions, we had all better beware." I am learning to expect questions I cannot answer—that's easy; I just say that I can't answer them. What is far more difficult is questions I would rather not answer.

A winter ago I had an after-school seminar for high-school students and in one of the early sessions Una, a brilliant fifteen-year-old, a born writer who came to Harlem from Panama five years ago, and only then discovered the conflict between races, asked me out of the blue: "Mrs. Franklin, do you really and truly believe in God with no doubts at all?"

"Oh, Una, I really and truly believe in God with all kinds of doubts."

But I base my life on this belief.

.. 21 ..

Una kept pushing me, wanting to know (I think wanting to be reassured) if I really believed in God. One day she brought it up at the beginning of the class, and the others seemed to want to talk too, so I plunged in: "There are three ways you can live life—three again—remember that the great writers almost always do things in threes. You can live life as though it's all a cosmic accident; we're nothing but an irritating skin disease on the face of the earth. Maybe you can live your life as though everything's a bad joke. I can't."

63

They couldn't, either, though for some of the kids who sat around the table that day not much had happened to make them think that life is anything else.

"Or you can go out at night and look at the stars and think, yes, they were created by a prime mover, and so were you, but he's aloof perfection, impassible, indifferent to his creation. He doesn't care, or, if he cares, he only cares about the ultimate end of his creation, and so what happens to any part of it on the way is really a matter of indifference. You don't matter to him, I don't matter to him, except possibly as a means to an end. I can't live that way, either."

Again there was general agreement.

"Then there's a third way: to live as though you believe that the power behind the universe is a power of love, a personal power of love, a love so great that all of us really *do* matter to him. He loves us so much that every single one of our lives has meaning; he really does know about the fall of every sparrow, and the hairs of our head are really counted. That's the only way I can live."

That seemed to make a certain amount of sense to them, so I thought that it was time to get down to the business of writing practices. Such discussions are inevitable in a writing seminar, and anything that stretches the mind is a help to the potential author. But my main job is to try to share the tools of the trade, so I said, "Now let's talk about punctuation. Punctuation is one of your chief tools in writing a story. I break the rules of punctuation over and over again, but before you may break a rule you must know what it is, and exactly why you're breaking it."

So we did a small run-down on punctuation, and I told them some of the devices I've found useful. When I'm giving conversation in the present I use a double quotation mark: ". When I'm giving conversation in the past of a story, I use a single quotation mark: '. And when I'm using interior conversation, interior monologue, I use the French symbol for conversation: —. This saves a lot of "he thought" and "she thought."

I love semicolons and colons. And punctuation serves to indicate rhythm. A semicolon is a longer pause than a comma, and a colon means really sitting back and taking note, but doesn't indicate a conclusion, like a period mark, or, as the English call it, a full stop.

Dashes should be used with respect. I seldom use them in a novel, except in conversation. I love them in letters. Exclamations and italics are like four-letter words, best used very sparingly.

Copy editors, except the present one at F S & G, who is an artist herself, are apt to monkey around with punctuation. You have to watch them like a hawk.

When *A Wrinkle in Time* went into galleys, the copy editor —I'm glad I haven't the faintest idea who it was—had him/herself a ball. First of all, I do spell the English way; I was in an English boarding school when I was twelve, thirteen, and fourteen, and these are the years when spelling gets set. After I had been made to write h-o-n-o-u-r, for instance, a hundred times on a blackboard several hundred times, it was almost impossible for me to spell it h-o-n-o-r. The English use t-o-w-a-r-d-s and we use t-o-w-a-r-d. I like to use them both, depending on the rhythm of the sentence and the letter which begins the following word; sometimes the *s* is needed; sometimes not: this is, I realize, rather erratic, and I can't blame the copy editor who tries to talk me out of it. Then there's *grey*, which is English, and one very definite, bird-wing, ocean-wave color to me; and *gray*, which is American, and a flatter, more metallic color. Then there are the *c* and *s* words, such as practice or practise. About words like these I'm simply in a state of confusion, rather than aesthetic persuasion, as with *grey* or *towards,* and the copy editor can have his way. On the whole I tell the copy editor to go ahead and make the spelling American, but don't muck around with the punctuation.

The worst thing the copy editor did with *A Wrinkle in Time* was with the three strange Mrs Ws. Now, Mr and Mrs are usually spelled Mr and Mrs in England, and Mr. and Mrs. in America. Usually I spell them the American way, or try to remember to. But the Mrs W were extra-special as well as extra-terrestrial, and I very deliberately did not put the period after their Mrs's. With Mr. and Mrs. Murry, who, scientists or no, were solid earth folk, I did put in the period. It was important to me. It was, I should have thought, obvious that it was done with forethought, but the copy editor went through the manuscript and put a period after every Mrs Whatsit, Mrs Who, and Mrs Which.

When I got the galleys I was appalled. I called my editor and told him what had happened. He was sorry, though certainly it was not a matter of vital import to him, as it was to me. He said, "If you insist, we'll take the periods out, but it will cost a fortune." If I insisted I would be acting like an impossible and temperamental author (I am convinced that I am the most gentle, pliable, easily managed author-wife-mother who ever walked the earth), and my editors would not be pleased. And they were taking a risk on a book that almost every other publisher in the business had turned down, and I was more than grateful. So I didn't insist. But it bothered me (it still does).

When the book was done in England, at last I was able to get the punctuation the way I wanted it: joy! though (temperamental author again?) I wasn't wholly satisfied on two counts: the publishers thought the book was too long for English children, and a few cuts were made; they weren't disastrous, but I think they shouldn't have been made; everything that could be cut had already been cut before the original publication. Then, I was asked if I would mind if the setting of the story were identified as being in America. I replied that I didn't think it was very important, but if they felt it to be essential, go ahead.

The first sentence of the book is very carefully and deliberately that old war-horse:

It was a dark and stormy night.

Period. End of sentence. End of paragraph.

The English edition begins, "It was a dark and stormy night in a small village in the United States."

I was naturally delighted when Penguin Publications decided to make a Puffin Book out of it. But lo, the Puffin copy editor took the periods out after Mr. and Mrs. Murry, too.

Ah, well.

TWO

How did we come to spend almost a decade year round at Crosswicks?

We bought the house a few months after we were married, for the astounding sum—astounding even a quarter of a century ago—of sixty-three hundred dollars. *Sic.* It was where we were going to sink our roots deep into the ground; it was our piece of land. I think it meant something unique to me because I had never before lived in a *house.* I was born in New York; we lived in an apartment. In Europe we lived in hotels, or *pensions,* or some kind of rented place which was not our own. When I got out of college I shared an apartment in Greenwich Village with three other girls, then moved to my own. Hugh and I started our married life in an apartment. But Crosswicks was a house, a real house. We planted trees, trees which would take an entire lifetime to mature. The great elms in front of the house, the bridal elms, had been planted as each of the original daughters of the house was married. Our trees, too, were an affirmation. This was where we wanted to raise our family—we hoped for six children.

Hugh was doing well in the theatre, but Crosswicks was too far to commute, and he loved Crosswicks. The spring before his thirty-fifth birthday—we had spent only summers in Crosswicks for the first years—he said that if he were ever to earn a living outside the theatre it would have to be at once, before he

was too old. Within a month of that pronouncement I was pregnant with our son, Bion, and this seemed to be the moment to
make the decision. But, we discovered, thirty-five is already too
old. Hugh had a degree in speech from Northwestern University, but he had no training or degree in engineering or business, which knocked out the possibility of a white-collar job.

So he decided he'd get a blue-collar job and applied at several
of the "shops" in Clovenford, the nearest town. When he was
given the routine tests he came out as a genius; he was told that
he couldn't possibly be put on a machine with that kind of rating. For a while we were near despair. But suddenly we found
ourselves the owners of the General Store, a run-down store in
the center of the village, the only store. The post office was in it,
and people used to pick up a loaf of bread when they got their
mail in the morning, or a pack of cigarettes when they got the
evening paper. But it had lots of potential. At first Hugh had
visions of an old-fashioned general store, with a cracker barrel
and jars of licorice sticks. But we aren't on the tourist route.
What was needed in the village was a plain, honest-to-goodness
grocery store, and if we were to make any kind of a living for
ourselves and our children, that was what we had to provide.

We did. Hugh, with no background whatsoever in this area
—an actor, from a family of lawyers—built up a splendid business; he wrote and mimeographed a weekly newspaper, giving
town news, meetings, birthdays, anniversaries, along with the
week's specials. The husband of the soprano with the most
beautiful voice in the choir needed a job, and they were talking
of leaving town: I couldn't bear losing that voice, so we took
Chuck on part-time, very shortly full-time, and within a year he
became our butcher, friend, and general uncle; we couldn't
have managed without him.

While the store was a-building, Hugh was happy. It was like

a Double-Crostic for him. But a business gets to a plateau; it reaches its peak, and there is no way to go further except to start another store. A chain of stores was hardly what Hugh really wanted. He'd made a success of one store, and that was enough. Our children were out of diapers, and we couldn't have any more babies, so one night I said, "Are you really still happy with the store?" "No. Not now." "Then sell it."

He had left the theatre forever. Forever lasted nine years. We learned a lot in those nine years, and we made friends who are definitely forever.

How to tell a little about those growing years? As I tell my students, one must particularize; show, do not tell. Perhaps if I remember the particular story of the Brechsteins, it will set, a little more clearly, the scene in which Grandma offered me her life.

Whenever anybody moves into a village as small as ours, it's a big event. We all live so close together, we know each other so well, that each new family can actively affect the climate of the town.

I was one of the first to see the Brechsteins. I was at the store as usual during the noon hour, and Wilberforce Smith came in for some teat dilators for his cows and asked if I'd seen the new people who'd bought the old Taylor house. And about an hour later Mrs. Brechstein came in.

She had on tight-fitting orange slacks in a day when women wore slacks because they were convenient to work in, not for chic: it was a little immoral to wear slacks for chic; Mrs. Brechstein's slacks were anything but practical. She wore them with a chartreuse shirt and dangly bronze earrings. Her two little boys had on shabby blue jeans and one of them had a hole in his T-shirt. It wasn't the kind of shabbiness we're used to in this village, where nobody has very much money but neither is anybody destitute. It was ostentatious. It was as much a costume as Mrs. Brechstein's orange pants.

All right, let's be honest. I didn't like her right from the start. There was the way she and the children were dressed—I dress oddly enough; I have a feeling I'm referred to in the village as "Poor Hugh Franklin's wife." There was the way she made me feel a failure; I had a book making the forlorn rounds of many publishing houses, and she managed to rub the rejections in, simply by constantly asking me about something I considered my own business. There was even the way she asked me if our eggs were fresh.

She went back to the meat department that first day, and I could hear her saying that she could get a certain cut of meat cheaper at the A & P. (How can any store with the glorious name of The Great Atlantic and Pacific Tea Company call itself the A & P?) As I was checking her out and putting her purchases in a bag I asked her how they were getting on, if they were getting settled, and if there was anything we could do to help them.

She smiled at me condescendingly and said that if she decided to pick up odds and ends at the store, it might be simpler for her to have a charge account. "The name is Brechstein, you know," she drawled, "and of course we're *so* often confused with the Chosen People, but I assure you that our credit rating is impeccable."

I told her, with what I thought was creditable mildness, that so was the credit of all our Jewish customers.

"But we don't happen to be Jewish," she said, smiling at me tolerantly, as though I hadn't been able to understand her in the first place.

"I'm so sorry," I murmured absently as I rang up the cash register.

As she left, Wilberforce Smith came in again, this time for cigars for himself, and bag balm for his cows, and accompanied by the second selectman, Harry Nottingham. "Seen the Jews who bought the old Taylor house?" Harry asked him.

"Ayeh."

"Putting in two new bathrooms," Harry said. "Must be mighty full of piss."

Well, you see, that's all part of it. I don't mean the Brechsteins. When Hugh and I first took over the General Store there weren't many people around who hadn't been born within ten miles of the Center. And we, like almost all the young couples who moved in shortly after the war, had a naïve idea, as we filled our houses with furniture and furnaces and families, joined the church and the P.T.A., that after a year or so we would no longer be considered newcomers but would be accepted as belonging to the village.

But there's a story, and I doubt if it's apocryphal, of the young couple who moved into a New England village with their infant son. The baby grew up there, lived and worked there, and died in his nineties. He had no immediate family, so the villagers gave him a splendid funeral and erected a monument to him on which they had inscribed: DEARLY BELOVED THOUGH A STRANGER AMONG US.

One day Mrs. Brechstein came into the store and said accusingly, "I hear there was a Republican caucus last night."

"Yes, I believe there was."

"Why weren't we told about it?"

"I suppose for the same reason that we weren't. They didn't want us to know."

"Why on earth wouldn't they want us to know?" It was obvious that she thought newcomers were a lot better qualified than the old Yankees to handle town government. I wasn't sure of that, being an apolitical creature, but I did want the opportunity to know what was going on.

Wilberforce Smith came in then to get his paper. "Ask Mr. Smith," I said. "He used to be a state senator."

So Mrs. Brechstein bustled up to him.

"It was posted on the door of the Town Hall," he growled.

"But who goes and looks at the door of the Town Hall?"

She had a point. When people want anything spread around the village, they don't post a minuscule sign on the door of the Town Hall, hidden by the shadows of the elms. They make three signs, one for the filling station, one for the firehouse, one for the store. I'd offered time and time again to make the signs for town meetings or caucuses.

When I wasn't asked, and blustered to Hugh about the comparative cleanness of Tammany Hall, he said, "Look at it their way. They don't want newcomers butting in and telling them how to run things. You can't blame them. Everybody hates change."

"I don't."

"Sure you do. Remember looking at the baby tonight and saying you hated having him change so quickly? Same difference. And around here everything had been going on peacefully for years and years, and suddenly after the war a lot of people move in who promptly have quantities of small children, and suddenly everybody has to shell out a lot of money for a new school, and taxes go up, and naturally everybody yaps."

He was tactful enough not to mention that his clumsy, five-foot-ten-inch wife, trying unsuccessfully in the store to learn to say "to-may-to" instead of "to-mah-to," reading Schopenhauer behind the counter, or writing in a journal between customers, must have seemed a very peculiar bird to the people who came in to our store.

76

"I think it's un-American," Mrs. Brechstein was saying to Wilberforce Smith. "Positively un-American."

Wilberforce Smith chewed on his cigar and narrowed his eyes. I thought maybe I was going to enjoy a good fight between the two of them, but Wilberforce shrugged and went out.

"I don't understand it," Mrs. Brechstein said. "I don't understand it at all."

I was really on her side, though I wasn't about to admit it. I tried to explain, sounding like a record of Hugh when he talks reasonably to me—something which is necessary far too often. "Well, you can't blame them for resenting it when people like us come along and buy up the big old houses for our families and then splash on fresh coats of white paint a lot of the old people can't afford, and put in flush toilets when they've struggled with outhouses, and buy automatic washing machines and dryers and dishwashers. And now a family has put in a swimming pool. There's been a lot of talk about that swimming pool."

"I don't see why there should be," Mrs. Brechstein said coldly, and I could see she didn't like being included in the "us."

It bothered me as much as it did Mrs. Brechstein. Because we heard plenty in the store. We got it from both sides. We heard people say to us in a perfectly friendly way that everything would be all right if it weren't for the newcomers; but they hadn't forgotten we were newcomers ourselves (my actor husband was a lot better at the role of country storekeeper than I was; he refers to it now as his "longest run"). In a store, of course, the customer is always right, and it was my husband's displeasure I had to live with if I lost my temper there, and not the person whose remarks rankled.

One weekend when the Brechsteins had been in their house for a little over a month, we were invited to dinner by the people with the pool. They lived quite near the Brechsteins, and my hostess told me she'd invited them too. "Aren't they just fascinating?" she asked me. "We're so lucky to have cultured people like that move into town."

Maybe I just see Mrs. Brechstein from the wrong side of the counter.

But that was the night that Mrs. Brechstein made the first of her famous remarks. We'd all been for a swim, and in spite of the warmth of the June evening a cool night breeze had come up, and all of us women congregated in the Pools' lovely bedroom were shivering as we rubbed ourselves down and dressed. We all knew each other pretty well, having moved into town at more or less the same time, and having served together on innumerable church and school committees. I don't think any of us is particularly prudish, but there was something a little too deliberate about the way Mrs. Brechstein walked around stark staring naked and then leaned her elbows on Mrs. Pool's bureau, looking at the pictures of the little Pools, and of Mr. Pool, most handsome in his navy lieutenant's uniform.

Mrs. Brechstein remarked to Mrs. Pool, "For a man who's spent most of his life selling insurance, your husband has quite an interesting mind." But that, though not exactly the epitome of tact, was not the famous remark. I finished dressing and turned to see Mrs. Brechstein, still naked, sitting on Mrs. Pool's bed and pulling one sheer stocking up onto one gloriously tanned leg. Her leg was not the only tanned part of her, and her body did not have the usual white areas.

"Of course every intelligent woman," she was saying, "should have at least one affair after she's married. How else can she possibly continue to interest her husband?"

The words fell like stones into troubled waters.

78

"Well!" Mrs. Pool exclaimed brightly. "Let's all go downstairs and have some dinner, shall we?"

The next day, almost everyone who was at the party happened to drop in at the store.

"Of course she didn't mean it."

"Oh, yes, she did, she meant every word."

"She was drunk, then."

"No, she wasn't. She was stone-cold sober."

"She drank like a fish."

"She can certainly hold it, you have to say that for her."

"I'm out of luck if that's the only way I can manage to hold on to *my* husband."

I got an earful.

A few days later I got a different kind of earful.

The Brechsteins, like everybody else in the village, new and old (except the Pools) took their children swimming in the pond. Sometimes the mothers swam, too, but most of the time they sat around and kept an eye on the kids and gossiped. If it didn't seem too unfriendly, I sat on a rock a few feet out in the pond and tried to write. And we all tried to welcome the Brechsteins and their two skinny little boys. When the boys threw stones, nobody liked it, but in all honesty the Brechsteins were not the only people around who did not believe in disciplining their kids. Even so, permissive upbringing, much as I disapprove of it, and allowing the tots to express themselves at all costs, seemed to sit even less well on the Brechsteins than on anybody else. However, the thing that stuck most in the craw was their response to such well-intentioned questions as:

"How are you enjoying life in the country?"

"Isn't it much pleasanter than life in the city?"

"Isn't it wonderful for the children here?"

The answers ran something like, "No, we much prefer the city to the country. The children have no cultural opportunities here. There are so few people one can talk with."

Naturally the next thing that happened was someone leaning across the counter saying, "So-and-so is sure the Brechsteins are Communists."

I suppose the same thing happens in many communities; I know it does. But our village is where I've witnessed it happening. The minute Wilberforce Smith and any of his friends and relatives don't like anything a new resident does, out comes the Communist label. Well: Hugh and I had had our share of this kind of gratuitous slander, and it made me feel for the Brechsteins, though it couldn't make me like them.

In the autumn with the start of the school year the Brechstein boys went to the village school; there were quite a few sharp comments about the Brechsteins' actually condescending to send their children to our public school; wouldn't have thought it would be good enough for them. Mrs. Brechstein spoke loudly on all matters at P.T.A. meetings, and Mr. Brechstein joined the volunteer firemen, though he wasn't wanted, which must have been unfortunately obvious. One of the most tactless things he did was to win enormously at the regular weekly firemen's poker game.

One evening about six-thirty, as I was waiting for Hugh to come home, and the children were setting the table, we heard the sickening wail of the fire siren. It was, fortunately, only a chimney fire, but the next morning it was all over town that Mr. Brechstein had been telling the firemen how to do everything. The worst thing about it, Mr. Pool reported, was that the man had some sensible ideas. The firemen had grudgingly followed them and hated him all the more for being right. But Wilberforce Smith leaned over the counter, talking to two of the farmers who happened to be in the store, and said, "Damn' interfering fool doesn't even know what he's talking about. I wouldn't raise a finger to help if his house burned down. Serve him right. We don't want newcomers telling us to do things we can do in our sleep."

The Brechsteins were, of course, atheists, but the little boys wanted to go to Sunday School with their friends, so the parents, after too many too public conversations on the subject, decided it wouldn't contaminate them permanently, and let them go. The next thing we knew, the Brechsteins were single-handedly going from door to door trying to raise money for the fire escape.

We'd all been working in our own quiet ways on that fire escape for some time. It bothered all of us that the inadequate Sunday School facilities, particularly the kindergarten and primary rooms, were fire traps, and we'd been working very hard trying to do something about it. Most New Englanders, including my husband, who may come from Oklahoma but fits well in the New England landscape, will not do today what can be done tomorrow, but we were beginning to make progress. The fire escape was going to be brought up again at the annual church meeting in January, and we all felt that the money would be appropriated and that perhaps we might even get somewhere on building a parish house with proper Sunday School facilities.

When Mr. Brechstein came to our house, full of zeal and enthusiasm and talked about the safety of the kiddies' bodies as well as their souls, I wanted to tell him, Listen, Mr. B., you've just killed all our chances of a fire escape. Don't you, with all your pretensions to intellect and knowledge of psychology, know that if you want to get something like this done in New England (and most likely in Oklahoma and Okinawa, in Nebraska and Nepal, in Georgia, U.S.A., and Georgia, U.S.S.R.)

you have to sell it to a couple of open-minded old residents and let *them* do the canvassing? But he was somehow so pathetically eager, and he looked, with his balding head with the curly dark hair over the ears, so like a spaniel, that I dug down into my pocketbook instead.

"Fire is something you can't be too careful about," Mr. Brechstein said. "Next week we're having our whole house re-wired as a precaution." He then told me that perhaps his wife might find time to read one of my little books when she had finished the stack of important novels by her bed.

Anyhow, most people forgot the fire escape and remembered the Brechsteins.

"I won't have that damned Communist telling me what to do."

"They ought to be driven out of town."

"They better watch out."

Of course Wilberforce Smith and his gang were behind most of the talk, or at least gave it the gentle push that was all that was needed to get it going, and if anybody had asked me whom I liked least, Mr. Brechstein or Wilberforce Smith, I'd have been hard put to it to decide.

One afternoon Mrs. Brechstein dropped into the store for some odds and ends, and nobody else happened to be there.

"Why," she demanded, looking me straight in the eye, "doesn't anybody like us?" I was too embarrassed to say anything. "No, please tell me. We both know it's true. I didn't expect to find intimate friends in a place like this, of course, but—"

"Well, maybe it's because you *did*n't expect to find friends," I said tentatively.

"But it's more than that. I can do without friends, with my

independent mind, but I don't understand the feeling of dislike we get everywhere we go."

"Well," I fumbled, "you know you've talked a good deal about how you bring your children up, about how you never tell them what to do but try unobtrusively to guide their minds to the right decisions? It might be better if you treated everybody else that way, too."

"What do you mean?" she demanded.

"People around here don't like being told what to do. It isn't just the fire escape. It's everything else. You tell us all how we should run our lives, what we should read and what we should think of what we read, and what kind of wall-paper we should use and what colors we should wear, and even who we should go to bed with."

"What do you mean by that last remark?" she snapped. And then to my horror a great tear slipped out of one eye and trick-led down her cheek. "Of course I know what you mean," she said. "I'd had too much to drink and I was scared out of my wits by all of you people who knew each other so well. And I *did* expect to make friends but I didn't know how. So I said it just to bolster my self-confidence. Of course I don't go around hav-ing affairs. I just thought it would make you—make you—" And she rushed out of the store and got in her car and drove off, leaving her bread on the counter.

I was appalled. And ashamed. Surely we should have real-ized. All that brashness. All that arrogance. Just a front, and one we should have been able to see through.

Hugh and I talked it over that evening. Mr. Brechstein had come to him, too, with complaints about the unfriendliness of New Englanders, their lack of hospitality, their suspicious na-tures.

"I don't think I'll ever really like them," I said, "but I do feel terribly sorry for them now. They've managed to hit me so often on my vulnerable spots that I never stopped to look at it from their point of view. Pretty Brechsteiny of me, wasn't it?"

Just after we had first fallen into sleep, that deep, heavy sleep out of which it is almost impossible to rouse, the fire siren started. The wild screech going up and down the scale, up and down, over and over, shattering the peace of the night, pierced insistently through my subconscious, until at last I was aware that I was listening to something. I lay there and started to shiver as I always do when I hear the siren. Up and down, on and on, over and over, the high, penetrating scream probed through sleep. I raised up on one elbow and looked over at Hugh, and he was still sound asleep.

—He's so tired, I thought, —he's been working so hard lately, I can't wake him.

I turned over on my side. Still the siren screamed. —Suppose it was our house, and somebody else's wife said to herself, My husband's so tired, I don't want to get him up to go out in the cold . . .

I took Hugh's shoulder and shook it gently. "Hugh. Hugh. It's the fire siren." He groaned and rolled over. "It's the fire siren," I said again.

Suddenly and all at once he was awake, swinging his legs out of bed, going to the south windows, then the east windows, standing with his bare feet on the ice-cold floor.

"It's in the center, and it's a big fire," he said suddenly, and started to dress.

"Please dress warmly," I begged. "I know you're rushing but please don't forget your boots. You won't be any help to anybody if you freeze." Do *all* men, if their wives don't plead with them, tend to dash out of the house in midwinter as though it were July?

I got out of bed and went to the window, and the east was lit with a great glow. I thought of all the houses in the center, but the bloody smear was so general that it was impossible to tell where the fire actually was. "It looks as though it might be the church," I said.

"If it is, thank God it's at a time when there's nobody in it." Hugh pulled a ski sweater over his head.

"And Mr. Brechstein will be right as usual." I tried to make myself smile. Hugh went downstairs and out into the dark, and I could hear the cold engine of the car cough as he started it. Before he was out of the garage there was the sound of another car hurrying down the road, and then another, from the two farms above us, and then Hugh was following them. I knew that I couldn't go to bed till he got home, so I pulled on my bathrobe and stood again at the east window looking at the horrible red glare. It was so violent that I could see bursts of flame thrusting flares up into the night. The phone rang and I ran to answer it. It couldn't be that something had happened to Hugh; he'd scarcely had time to get to the center.

It was my neighbor up the road. "Madeleine, do you know where the fire is?"

"No. It's in the center. It looks as though it might be the church. Has Howard gone?"

"Ayeh. If you hear where it is, call me, will you?"

"Yes, and same to you, please." I was too nervous to sit down, to read, to try to write. I went to the kitchen and put the kettle on for tea, then went upstairs and checked the children, tucked them in, walked our little boy to the bathroom, tidied up some clothes that had fallen on the closet floor, picked up Raggedy

Ann and tucked her back in beside a small sleeping girl, went back down to the kitchen and drank a cup of tea. There was no possible hope that those flames might be from a chimney fire. I thought of the church, the beautiful church, well over two hundred years old, with the tall white spire visible for miles, with the bell that could be heard for miles too, that tolled for the hours, for births, weddings, deaths.

I looked in the refrigerator to see what I could make into a sandwich for Hugh when he got home. The phone again: my neighbor: "Madeleine, it's not the church. It's down the hill to Brechsteins'."

'I wouldn't raise a finger,' Wilberforce Smith had said, 'if his house burned down.' There had even been some wild talk about burning those Commies out.

The phone again. It would wake the children. But no, the fire alarm had not penetrated their sleep; it would take more than the phone to rouse the children. "It's the Brechsteins'," I was able to say this time.

It takes more than the scream of a fire siren, more than the insistent ring of the phone, to rouse the children. Were those little beasts the Brechstein boys all right? Little beasts or no, the thought of a child in a burning house is an unbearable one. I rushed upstairs to stand looking at our own children, lying safe and sweet in their beds. Naughty and noisy as they might be by day, at night they looked like cherubs; all children do, and I was sure the Brechstein boys were no exception.

My neighbor rang again. "It's the wing of the house. Not a chance of saving it, but they might be able to save the main house."

The wing. The wing was where the boys' bedroom was.

If it weren't for our sleeping children, how many of us would have followed our men over to the fire? We were thinking of the Brechstein boys; we were thinking of our men trying to fight the flames; none of us, native or newcomer, could stop our nervous pacing, and the phone was our only relief from the tension.

"Those boys sleep in the wing."

"Yes. I know."

"Do you suppose they're all right?"

"My Johnny gave Peter Brechstein a bloody nose in school today. The kid asked for it, but now—"

"They've called the Northridge fire department, too."

"Yes, and Clovenford."

I drank another cup of tea. I checked on the children once more. I stood at the window and the glare had died down. There was no longer the bright bursting of flames, and the sky looked only murky and sick, and at last I realized that part of the light was coming from dawn.

A car came up the road, and then another, and then the kitchen door opened and I ran to meet Hugh. His face was black with soot and he looked exhausted. While I fixed him something to eat and drink he began to tell me about it. "It was the wing of the Brechsteins' house. Burned clear down. But they saved the main house. Couldn't possibly have done it if everybody hadn't got there so quickly."

"But the boys, what about the boys?" I asked.

"Wilberforce Smith went in after them," Hugh told me. "Burned his hands badly, too, but the boys weren't touched."

Relief surged through me. "No one was really hurt?"

"No. Everybody's okay. Mr. Brechstein worked like a madman. Everybody did."

"You included," I said.

"A lot of them are still there. Don't dare leave while it's still smoldering."

"How did the fire start?"

"Nobody knows for sure. Probably faulty wiring." He stretched and yawned.

"Try to get a nap," I begged, "before time to get up."

A nap, of course, was all it was, hardly even that, because we simply lay in our big bed holding each other, taking comfort in touch, the beating of the heart, the gentle motion of breath, holding each other in the manner of the human being in time of danger, sorrow, death.

Then there was the usual rush of getting the children ready for school, Hugh off for the store, and then the phone started ringing, and we were all off in a mad whirl of baking pies and cakes for the men still working in the debris of what had been the long white wing of the house, and collecting clothes for the Brechsteins, and cleaning up the main house so that there was no sign of smoke or water or broken windows, and for a few splendid days thousands of cups of coffee were swallowed and all the tensions were miraculously eased, and the church women held a kitchen shower for the Brechsteins because the kitchen had been in the wing, and Mrs. Brechstein managed not to put her foot in her mouth, and people forgot for an evening who was old and who was new and nobody called anybody else a Communist. It was at least a week before somebody came into the store and said angrily, "Did you hear what the Brechsteins did *now?*"

Perhaps New Englanders are unfriendly, and perhaps I'll never understand or like either the Brechsteins or Wilberforce Smith, and perhaps we'll never feel anything but newcomers in this tight little community.

But where, after we have made the great decision to leave the security of childhood and move on into the vastness of maturity, does anybody ever feel completely at home?

Children and grownups ask me the same questions about my stories, though children, less inhibited, ask more: How old are you? How much money do you make?

One standard question from young and old is: Do you write about real people, and about what really happened?

The answer is no. But also yes. My husband says, and I'm afraid with justification, that by the time I've finished a book I have no idea what in it is fabrication and what is actuality; and he adds that this holds true not only for novels but for most of my life. We do live, all of us, on many different levels, and for most artists the world of imagination is more real than the world of the kitchen sink.

When my mother apologizes for the many things that gave me a childhood that was rather different from the normal, happy, American ideal, I try to convince her of my immense gratitude. She at least has to admit that I've got a lot of material for a lot of books out of it, because every single one of my adolescent heroines is based on my own experience.

When someone comes in to me when I'm deep in writing, I have a moment of frightening transition when I don't know where I am, and then I have to leave the "real" world of my story for what often seems the less real world, the daily, dearly loved world of husband and children and household chores.

Perhaps the story of the Brechsteins will help sort things out. There are, in one sense, no Brechsteins. I think I made the name up. If we must be psychoanalytical about why I made up that particular name, it was, I fancy, because I was having trouble with my piano—keys stuck, strings broke—and I dreamed of a Steinway or a Bechstein grand. Their story is just one of a series of sketches I wrote one winter of inner and outer cold, and it's hardly even a story. I wrote it over a decade ago, while we were still living year round in the country, so I'm more able to be objective about it than something written more recently, and it is, in its setting, more overtly autobiographical than most of my stories.

But with this sketch, as with all my stories, the idea simply comes to me and asks to be written; all I am aware of, on the conscious level of writing, is the story, and the imaginary people in it, and if I have, in fact, written from "real life" I'm usually not aware of it for months—or years.

All right. Our house is our house. The store is our store. My husband and I are ourselves. The emotional premise of the sketch, the feeling of being a stranger and sojourner—all this is true. This is the way it is. We did have a difficult time getting a fire escape for the second floor of the church, though probably most of us have forgotten it by now; it's only this story which makes me remember it, and I haven't thought about it for years, or how desperately important it was to us then.

We also have a parish house, and notices for town meetings and caucuses are posted where everybody will see them. But there will always, I suspect, be a line, bridgeable but always there, between old and new members in every small community.

There is no Wilberforce Smith. He is totally unlike the two fine first selectmen we have known since we bought Crosswicks. If I try hard to pin him down, he might be a mixture of two or three different people who came into the store, but I'm not really sure, and from my point of view it doesn't matter, because who he is is Wilberforce Smith.

As for the Brechsteins, there was a new family in town, from Chicago, who were resented and called Communists because they tried to push World Federalism at a time when an interest in the United Nations was considered un-American. Then there was another family, in the village for one summer only, a mother, father, and barely adolescent girl. The wife had written a scholarly book on the number of times contemporary writers use eight-letter words (or something like that; she used a computer); the husband was a sociologist. We had been asked to be nice to them, to help them feel at home, and I looked forward to someone who might enjoy talking about writing and music.

They turned out to be Brechsteiny, all right. Our girls and their friends finally stopped trying to get along with the "Brechstein" girl, and I thought they were noble to try as long as they did. Mrs. Brechstein certainly made me feel obvious, to say the least. I was not, she made it clear, her intellectual equal, and when she pontificated about her book she bored me, and everybody else. Mr. Brechstein looked down on Hugh for running a grocery store. I think that Mrs. Brechstein actually did make the famous remark about the necessity for a wife to have an affair, but I'm not sure. At the end of the summer they left the village and our lives, and I wish them well.

The fire siren always sends chills of terror through me. There was a night when it blew, when I did not want to pry Hugh out of his needed sleep, when the sky to the east was lit with flame and we did not know, for a long time, where the fire was, when it might have been the church, or any of the houses in the center, when I did all the things that the me of the Brechstein sketch did. It was not a house, after all, but a barn; bad enough, for the loss of a barn is disastrous for a farmer; and not all the cows were saved.

In writing about the Brechsteins I was writing about all kinds of things which were on my mind, my conscious, sub-, and super-conscious mind. After I had finished it, and the story itself reminded me that we are all strangers and sojourners on this earth, I was far more reconciled to not knowing about a Republican caucus than I had been before—though it didn't stop me from trying to make such meetings generally known. I have my own idea of what is American.

A note about our village here, our beloved village which can always be counted on to come through in time of crisis. Maybe Wilberforce Smith is everybody who makes me angry with self-centered narrow-mindedness and then undoes me utterly by an act of selfless nobility, such as Wilberforce going into the burning house for the little boys. When Senator Joe McCarthy began making his Communist accusations on television, we thought we'd hear a lot of pro-McCarthy talk in the store: but no: the Yankee sense of fair play came to the fore. McCarthy had gone too far. For a long time after his obscenities there were no more accusations around here of Communism.

A village is very much like boarding school (I was in boarding schools for ten years, so I know whereof I talk): let any threat come from outside, and everybody, old and new, Republican and Democrat, white-collar worker or blue, will band together.

Perhaps that is what our divided world needs now: a threat from outside. Certainly, as one good American said, if we do not hang together we will hang separately.

.. 3 ..

Thinking about the Brechsteins, attempting the not-quite possible task of separating fact from fiction in this sketch, teaches me something about the nature of reality. On one level, one might say that the Brechsteins are not real. But they are. It is through the Brechsteins, through the world of the imagination which takes us beyond the restrictions of provable fact, that we touch the hem of truth. The world we live in, the world we are able to know with our intellect, is limited and bounded by our finiteness. We glimpse reality only occasionally, and for me it happens most often when I write, when I start out using all the "real" things which my senses and my mind can know, and then suddenly a world opens before me.

Reality: I can only affirm that the people in my stories have as complete and free a life of their own as do my family and friends; to the extent that they become alive for the reader, the story has succeeded. For me, this says a lot about the nature of reality.

The only inadvertent exceptions I've made to my usual unknowing where or from whom my characters spring, are Rob Austin, who simply is our youngest child, and there's nothing I can do about it; and Canon Tallis, who walked, unexpected, into J.F.K. Airport when Adam Eddington was waiting to fly to Lisbon. If I tried consciously to write about an actual person, I would be limited by that person; the character could not do anything that the person, as far as I understand him, would not do. But an imaginary character is not limited; he does and says all kinds of things I don't expect, and often don't want. When a character wants to do one thing and I want him to do another, the character is usually right.

But I don't suppose it's possible for a writer to create a wholly imaginary character. Whether we are aware of it or not, we are drawing from every human being we have ever known, have passed casually in the street, sat next to on the subway, stood behind in the check-out line at the supermarket. Perhaps one might say that we draw constantly from our subconscious minds, and undoubtedly this is true, but more important than that is the super-conscious level which comes to our aid in writing—or painting or composing—or teaching, or listening to a friend.

When I was writing *The Arm of the Starfish*, I had the story thoroughly plotted, and there was no Joshua Archer in it. Nevertheless, when Adam Eddington woke up in the Ritz Hotel in Lisbon, there was a young man sitting in his room, a young man named Joshua Archer, and Joshua was as much of a surprise to me as he was to Adam, and he changed the plot radically. He made me rewrite at least half the book.

But I do have to know, with all five senses, the places in which these unpredictable people move. When I was working on the story of Mariana Alcoforado, the Portuguese nun, I realized that I couldn't possibly get really deep into it until I had been to Portugal, to Beja, where Mariana's convent was, until I had touched, tasted, smelled, heard, seen. I had been thinking of Portugal as something like the South of France, which I knew with my senses, but I was aware that this wasn't good enough. When some movie money came through, Hugh said, "All right, now we'll go to Portugal."

We left two days after Christmas, sending our children back here to stay with friends. We were in Portugal ten days, ten intensely profitable days, because I got two books out of it, *The Love Letters* and *The Arm of the Starfish*. Our plane, like Adam's, could not land in Lisbon because of the fog, and went on to Madrid; like Adam, we spent the day in the Prado. We, too, took a bumpy Caravelle back to Lisbon. We stayed in the Ritz for two nights, so I knew what that room where Joshua appeared was like. On our way back from the south of Portugal we stayed at the Avenida Palace, where Adam went after Poly had disappeared from the Caravelle; the room in which Dr. O'Keefe told him to wait was the room in which we stayed.

During those ten days I wrote over two hundred pages of journal.

"Turn out the light," Hugh would sometimes say, testily.

"I can't, I haven't got it all down yet."

"Write it tomorrow."

"I can't, I have to do it now, while it's still alive."

He is very good about understanding, and even encouraging, this.

.. 4 ..

An author is responsible for his characters in much the same way that a parent is for his children, or a teacher for his students. Sometimes this manifold responsibility weighs heavily on me; I want to retreat entirely, lest I do damage. But we have to accept the stark fact that we not only can but inevitably will do damage. It's that Omaha psychiatrist versus George Mac-Donald, perhaps?

At a meeting of the Children's Book Committee of the Authors Guild a couple of winters ago, we had a hot argument about this. The kind of responsibility I'm thinking about is both difficult and dangerous, especially where it affects children. But we're living in a difficult and dangerous world, and no amount of sticking our heads in the sand is going to make it any easier. Western man has tried for too many centuries to fool himself that he lives in a rational world. No. There's a story about a man who, while walking along the street, was almost hit on the head and killed by an enormous falling beam. This was his moment of realization that he did not live in a rational world but a world in which men's lives can be cut off by a random blow on the head, and the discovery shook him so deeply that he was impelled to leave his wife and children, who were the major part of his old, rational world. My own response to the wild unpredictability of the universe has been to write stories, to play the piano, to read, listen to music, look at paintings—not that the world may become explainable and reasonable but that I may rejoice in the freedom which unaccountability gives us.

We sat there in the Authors Guild, looking out the windows to a stricken city, paralyzed at that time by a strike of fuel-oil deliverers in the midst of a flu epidemic; people were dying because of this strike, dying for fringe benefits, mostly people in the ghetto parts of the city where landlords don't care whether the buildings are heated or not. Only a short while behind us—and ahead of us—were other strikes, garbage-collector strikes (we keep having these, and the city gets more and more attractive to rats, rodent and human); student strikes; teacher strikes; phone-company strikes; welfare-recipient strikes; transit strikes; you name it, we've had it—or we will have it. I sometimes wonder if the ancient Romans were as aware of their crumbling civilization as we New Yorkers can't help being of ours; did they, too, sometimes sit around a candlelit dinner table with friends, and wonder how many times they would be able to meet thus; did they, too, draw closer together because of the anger and dark outside?

We, of the Children's Book Committee, sat in our pleasant skyscraper room and discussed a possible program for the next meeting of the Guild. I suggested that we ask each other, "What is the responsibility of the writer today?"

Someone asked—I think it was Ann Petry or Elizabeth George Speare, two of the writers I most admire: "Do you mean as a person or as a writer?"

I tried to explain that I, for one, was not separable. I can't, as I think I've made plain, be pulled apart like a jigsaw puzzle that can be dismantled and then put back together again. I am, for better or worse, writer, wife, mother, and all these bits of me are inseparably blended to make up the human being who is—or who is not—responsible.

"But books are a story," someone else said. "That's what they have to be: entertainment. They shouldn't be anything else."

Well, of course. The story comes, and it is pure story. That's all I set out to write. But I don't believe that we can write any kind of story without including, whether we intend to or not, our response to the world around us.

The writing of a book may be a solitary business; it is done alone. The writer sits down with paper and pen, or typewriter, and, withdrawn from the world, tries to set down the story that is crying to be written. We write alone, but we do not write in isolation. No matter how fantastic a story line may be, it still comes out of our response to what is happening to us and to the world in which we live.

Last summer in England, when I was talking at the college where Alan is teaching, someone said, "But what about the mystery writers? They don't make any response to the problems of the world in their stories." And I cried, "Oh, but they do!" and cited some of my favorite writers, Josephine Tey, John Dickson Carr, Dorothy Sayers—I could go on and on—and said, "Think about them. Their mysteries may be nothing but exciting stories on the surface, but there's a definite moral response to the world in every single one of the really good ones."

It wasn't till this summer that it occurred to me that most of my favorite mystery writers are English, and use the language literately; their syntax is not an insult to the reader. Even more important, most of them write out of a belief in a universe created by a God of love.

Something odd and sad: I originally wrote that many of my

favorite mystery writers were practicing Christians, and two people whose opinion I respect told me that the word "Christian" would turn people off. This certainly says something about the state of Christianity today. I wouldn't mind if to be a Christian were accepted as being the dangerous thing which it is; I wouldn't mind if, when a group of Christians meet for bread and wine, we might well be interrupted and jailed for subversive activities; I wouldn't mind if, once again, we were being thrown to the lions. I do mind, desperately, that the word "Christian" means for so many people smugness, and piosity, and holier-than-thouness. Who, today, can recognize a Christian because of "how those Christians love one another"?

No wonder our youth is confused and in pain; they long for God, for the transcendent, and are offered, far too often, either piosity or sociology, neither of which meets their needs, and they are introduced to churches which have become buildings that are a safe place to go to escape the awful demands of God.

As for the mystery writers, I stand by what I said: no one whose life is not based on the faith that the universe is in the hands of a responsible God would dare to become so intimately involved with death, and the evil in men's hearts.

To be responsible means precisely what the word implies: to be capable of giving a response. It isn't only the Flower Children or Hell's Angels who are opting out of society. A writer who writes a story which has no response to what is going on in the world is not only copping out himself but helping others to be irresponsible, too. I mentioned that all of us on the Children's Book Committee *do* give our response to the world around us in our books, even if only by implication. I brought up several books written by the members of the committee, books which are perfect examples of the kind of responsibility I am talking about, and added, "You're my friends, and you've read *The Young Unicorns* [it had recently been published]; you know there's more than just the story. If what I have to say is right, or if it is wrong, I'm responsible for it, and I can't pretend that I'm not, just because it's difficult."

To refuse to respond is in itself a response. Those of us who write are responsible for the effect of our books. Those who teach, who suggest books to either children or adults, are responsible for their choices. Like it or not, we either add to the darkness of indifference and out-and-out evil which surround us or we light a candle to see by.

We can surely no longer pretend that our children are growing up into a peaceful, secure, and civilized world. We've come to the point where it's irresponsible to try to protect them from the irrational world they will have to live in when they grow up. The children themselves haven't yet isolated themselves by selfishness and indifference; they do not fall easily into the error of despair; they are considerably braver than most grownups. Our responsibility to them is not to pretend that if we don't look, evil will go away, but to give them weapons against it.

One of the greatest weapons of all is laughter, a gift for fun, a sense of play which is sadly missing from the grownup world. When one of our children got isolated by a fit of sulks, my husband would say very seriously, "Look at me. Now, don't laugh. Whatever you do, don't laugh." Nobody could manage to stay long-faced for very long, and communication was reestablished. When Hugh and I are out of sorts with each other, it is always laughter that breaks through the anger and withdrawal.

Paradox again: to take ourselves seriously enough to take ourselves lightly. If every hair of my head is counted, then in the very scheme of the cosmos I matter; I am created by a power who cares about the sparrow, and the rabbit in the snare, and the people on the crowded streets; who calls the stars by name. And you. And me.

When I remember this it is as though pounds were lifted from me. I can take myself lightly, and share in the laughter of the white china Buddha on my desk.

.. 5 ..

A spring ago, on the Sunday which in the calendar of the church is called Pentecost, the young people's group conducted the worship service. The church stands in the center of the village, a white colonial building with pillars, a proper fire escape, and a tall spire; someone once told me that it is the tallest spire in the state. The interior, alas, was redone during the worst excesses of Victorianism, but it is still a dignified and austere place of worship.

The young people started their service with a pop record about the need for love to conquer hate. As the record played, they danced in the chancel, improvising their steps and movements to what each one felt the record was saying. I was sitting towards the front, but the sense of shock behind me was tangible. I didn't need to turn around to realize that at least one person was getting up and walking out. When the record was over, one of the girls, a senior in high school, went to the lectern and told us that the Pilgrim Fellowship was not there to shock the congregation but to try to explain what was on their minds, to try to communicate to the grownups what they were feeling. And she talked about the importance of being an individual. She cared passionately.

I had sung with this girl's mother in choir. I had felt a helpless anguish when the oldest little girl, who should now be in college, died of cancer. What was being said from the lectern by this high-school senior came from everything her growing up had taught her. But someone else left the church.

Then one of the boys came forward. His mother, too, had been in the choir; we had carried our youngest children at the same time. I had watched him learn to walk and talk; our boys have been friends all their lives. What he had to say on this Pentecost was that he was no longer able to believe in the god who is talked about in church and Sunday School. If he was to believe in God, he had to find him in people, and he found him when he walked alone in the woods. Someone else walked out.

Then our nearest neighbor's boy, our son's close friend, came forward. He talked about war, and killing, and napalm bombs and burning babies and killing, killing, killing, and more people left.

Then the young people, still trying, came down into the congregation to pass the peace, the old tradition of the early centuries, where each person in the congregation turns to his neighbor, takes his hand, or embraces him, saying, "Peace be with you."

But by then the abyss between adolescent and adult was too great to be bridged.

On the first Pentecost, people of many races and languages were together, and each spoke in his own tongue, and everybody was able to understand everybody else. And here we were on Pentecost two thousand years later and there had been no understanding at all.

Most of the village was as much shocked by the lack in communication as by what some considered irreverence on the part of the young people. For the rest of the spring and summer Quinn held open meetings every other Sunday evening, where the generations could get together to try to communicate. This isn't always easy, and it isn't only the middle-aged who refuse to listen, who will not even try to understand another point of view. One boy would not get it through his head that for all adults God is not necessarily an old man in a white beard and nightgown sitting on a cloud. As far as this boy was concerned, this old gentleman was the adult's god, and therefore he did not believe in God. There were some parents who felt that love of country implies no freedom to criticize the country; I wonder if they also felt that to criticize or attempt to correct their children meant that they did not love them? This isn't what love means.

But at least people came to these meetings; they tried; and we got enough laughter out of the extremists—who didn't like being thought amusing—so that the laughter itself helped us knock down walls. And our varied languages were no longer quite so incomprehensible.

.. 6 ..

Last spring I conducted a seminar through the auspices of the P.E.N. and the Cathedral. The seminar was black, Wasp, Jew, Oriental, and this is the way I most like it to be, for this very diversity helps break down prejudice; if I—inevitably—become involved with the members of a seminar, so do they with each other. It wasn't long before we all knew each other by name, which meant that Una was Una first and black and militant second; that Jock was Jock first and privileged and Wasp second; that he could say, after hearing Una read a tragic story out of her own experience, "Una, I really envy you; that's awful, all that, but it makes me realize how sheltered I've been." Una, in her turn, for the first time saw some of her experiences as valuable in her understanding of herself and the world around her, saw and felt the extraordinary hope that comes from experience which comes from tribulation. We all asked, "Why is it that we learn from the things which hurt us? Why do we need pain before we can grow?" There aren't any easy answers to this one, but all artists know the truth of it, and not only artists: it was Jung who said that there is no coming to life without pain.

I learned from Una, from Jock, from all of them. One of the best things about these kids is that they don't worry about hurting any adult's feelings when they talk about the world we've made for them to live in. We've made a mess of it, there's no evading that. Nevertheless, no matter what we think of our educational system, more people today are literate than ever before. On the whole, even in desperate areas of poverty, most children have access to television sets, which—despite the mediocrity of many programs—give them a more sophisticated knowledge of what is going on in all corners of the world than any previous generation ever had. Because of our extraordinary technological advances in the last few decades, more opportunities are open to more young people than ever before.

But talk with them. What have we educated them for? Have we given them too heavy a diet materially and neglected them spiritually? They have a sense of eschatology (another of those *ology* words: the word about the end of time, the word about the last things) that my generation, even growing up into the Second World War, didn't experience. This spring our eleventh-grade son, calling home from boarding school, kept saying, "I don't have time," which is how many young people feel: if they aren't killed in a war which they don't understand, they'll die of lung cancer from the polluted environment, or radiation effects from milk containing Strontium 90, or simply rainfall or snowfall.

There was one snowfall at the Cathedral this winter which was a horrifying illustration of our ecology. I spend eight hours a day in the library of the Cathedral; I wandered in several years ago to write—there were too many disturbances at home —and became librarian by default. I have no qualifications, but I had no qualifications as choir director, either. And it is a perfect place for me, a big room full of books, including a splendid reference section; bay windows looking across the Close to the Cathedral itself; and an aura which says to me: Write.

Una, when asked to describe the library, where we held our seminar sessions, wrote, "When I walk in here I feel I can be myself." So do I. And it is run on the academic year, so I am free for our Crosswicks summers.

Back to the snowfall and ecology: I am allowed to bring my dogs to work with me. They lie quietly on a blanket by my desk; they are obedient and know that they are not allowed to jump up when someone comes in; and most people love them almost as much as I do. Just outside the library is a large fenced-in stretch of greensward, known as the Canon's Green, where all the Cathedral dogs romp. My dogs have many friends: Monarch, the bishop's corgi; Cynthia's two dachshunds; and Oliver and Tyrrell's greatest friend is Fritz, Tallis's Weimaraner, the size of a great Dane.

On the afternoon after this particular snowfall, Fritz and Tyrrell had a glorious time romping, taking great bites of snow, throwing it at each other, rolling in it. Oliver, our ancient collie, now dead of dignified old age, was feeling much too arthritic to do anything but stand and watch tolerantly. Later in the afternoon Tyrrell vomited, and so did Fritz. Tallis called our veterinary friend, who said that it was the snow; he'd had any number of calls from people complaining that their dogs had been throwing up. I told my husband when I got home that evening, and he said, "Last night when I was in Riverside Park walking the dogs, the snow looked so pure and beautiful that I held up my face and opened my mouth to it. How horrible to think that we can't do that any more."

Our children used to eat the snow when they were little, here at Crosswicks (maybe it's still all right here); we made toffee in it. Is Josephine going to have to say to her babies, "Be careful not to get the snow in your mouth, it might kill you"?

This sense of urgency has always been with my children, and those I work and talk with. They've grown up knowing that at any moment we could blow up our planet if some madman pushes the wrong button. During the Cuban crisis, when our youngest child was a second grader, we were listening to the news and when the weather report was announced he said, "Storms tomorrow. If there is a tomorrow."

Children, not without reason, blame the adults. But they want to talk about it with us, which is, in itself, an advance and a development. I know that I'm lucky when we talk, because the fact that they've read my books and responded to them means that walls between us are already down. During my happy day at Sidwell Friends School, several of the high-school students said to me, "We can't talk to our parents because they don't remember what it was like to be our age."

Memory is one of the most essential of the writer's tools, and a writer finds it easy to have total recall, just as other people find it easy to balance a checkbook—something entirely beyond my capacity. But the adolescents today are concerned over a general lack of memory in their parents and teachers, and it is this forgetfulness of what it is like to be twelve, or seventeen, or twenty-one, that is largely responsible for the famous generation gap. The young look at the amnesiac over-thirties and say, "We look at the adults around us, and if this is what it means to be grownup, then we say, No! We don't ever want to be like most of the adults we see."

So they dress as differently from us as they possibly can; they wear wild hairdos and symbolic jewelry; in a secular world they are crying out for transcendence; they try to get our attention in the most extreme ways; if we don't listen, they throw a bomb.

Una and I talked about this. She allied herself with the militants, and yet, with her open, loving face she talked to me about it. I said one day, "I can see you getting frustrated enough to throw a bomb, Una, but I can't see you throwing it in a building with anybody in it." We both did a lot of thinking about how far frustration can legitimately push us.

So the challenge I face with children is the redemption of adulthood. We must make it evident that maturity is the fulfillment of childhood and adolescence, not a diminishing; that it is an affirmation of life, not a denial; that it is entering fully into our essential selves.

I don't go along with the people who say they'd never want to live their childhoods again; I treasure every bit of mine, all the pains as well as the joy of discovery. But I also love being a grownup. To be half a century plus is wonderfully exciting, because I haven't lost any of my past, and am free to stand on the rock of all that the past has taught me as I look towards the future.

The youngsters' rejection of adults often shocks us so much that we in turn reject the rejection and are angered at the violent means by which they repudiate parents and teachers. They drop out of school and college because it just doesn't seem worthwhile. Or they want a college degree without having to work for it. Or they have trial marriages, or just share a pad, rather than entering into relationships which are intended to last for life, often following the example of parents who have separated or divorced, with the concomitant philosophy that if you try marriage and it doesn't work, you quit. They are rebelling not against our morality and discipline but against our lack of morality and our lack of discipline. They are unwilling to commit themselves with promises of fidelity in relationships because they have known too many grownups make these promises and then break them as though they didn't matter. Somehow or other, promises, as well as adulthood, must be redeemed. My seminar students asked me, "But isn't it better not to make the promises at all? Isn't it more honest?"

I shook my head. "No. I don't think so. And I think I do have a right to talk to you about this, because I've been married to the same man for almost twenty-five years, and we love each other more now than we did twenty-five years ago. When we were married we made promises, and we took them seriously. No relationship between two people which is worth anything is static. If a man and wife tell me they've never had a quarrel, I suspect that something is festering under the skin. There've been a number of times in my marriage when—if I hadn't made promises—I'd have quit. I'm sure this is equally true of Hugh; I'm not an easy person to live with."

I'm quite sure that Hugh and I would never have reached the relationship we have today if we hadn't made promises. Perhaps we made them youthfully, and blindly, not knowing all that was implied; but the very promises have been a saving grace.

It is generally accepted that youngsters, and not only those from the inner city but also those from the affluent suburbs and exurbs, are experimenting with sex and drugs, hard drugs. One bitter reason is that our country in general assumes that "the pursuit of happiness" really means "the pursuit of pleasure" and that therefore pleasure is the greatest good. For every discomfort there is a pill. Half the ads in our glossy magazines are for hard liquor: You're depressed? Get sloshed; feel good. Drink this, eat that, swallow the other, and your sex appeal will rise. Stay young, don't grow up, avoid contamination with death: have fun, fun, fun.

If pleasure is the greatest good, then why not seek it in drugs?

Another cause is the need of the human being for loyalty. Where home loyalties are lost, the drug subculture is an alternative. With the breakdown of close-knit family life, kids are desperately searching for new relationships. Small houses with no room for grandparents or stray aunts and uncles; fathers whose jobs keep them on the move—all this, as well as the shattering of families by divorce, has denied children the security of growing up in a close family unit, and they have to search desperately for another group to which they can be committed. There is no lack of commitment in the Black Panthers, or the Young Lords, or even Hell's Angels.

Then there's the need for adventure; we're not providing legitimate adventure for many of them: how many ghetto high-school kids can qualify for the Peace Corps or Vista? so they seek adventure illegitimately.

There have been a number of times during the past years when one of my "children" has come into the library, puttered around the bookshelves until we were alone, and then sat by my desk to talk about love: should I sleep with him? does he love me? is this girl just having me on? what do you really think about marriage? every boy you go out with expects you to make out, all the way; the girls want anything they can get out of you, but I think this one is different; how do you know if you're pregnant? my parents don't like her, they think she's a tramp, but she isn't, and I love her.

They really don't want me to answer their questions, nor should I. If I have not already answered them ontologically, nothing I say is going to make any sense. Where I can be of use is in being willing to listen while they spread their problem out between us; they can then see it themselves in better perspective.

But over the years two questions of mine have evolved which make sense to me.

I ask the boy or girl how work is going: Are you functioning at a better level than usual? Do you find that you are getting more work done in less time? If you are, then I think that you can trust this love. If you find that you can't work well, that you're functioning under par, then I think something may be wrong.

A lovely example of this is Josephine: the spring she and Alan were engaged, when she was eighteen and a sophomore at Smith, they found out that they could not possibly be apart more than two weeks at a time; either Alan would go up to Northampton, or Josephine would come down to New York.

She knew that she would be getting married ten days after the close of college. And her grades went steadily up.

The other question I ask my "children" is: what about your relations with the rest of the world? It's all right in the very beginning for you to be the only two people in the world, but after that your ability to love should become greater and greater. If you find that you love lots more people than you ever did before, then I think that you can trust this love. If you find that you need to be exclusive, that you don't like being around other people, then I think that something may be wrong.

This doesn't mean that two people who love each other don't need time alone. Two people in the first glory of new love must have great waves of time in which to discover each other. But there is a kind of exclusiveness in some loves, a kind of inturning, which augurs trouble to come.

Hugh was the wiser of the two of us when we were first married. I would have been perfectly content to go off to a desert isle with him. But he saw to it that our circle was kept wide until it became natural for me, too. There is nothing that makes me happier than sitting around the dinner table and talking until the candles are burned down.

I have been wondering this summer why our love has seemed deeper, tenderer than ever before. It's taken us twenty-five years, almost, but perhaps at last we are willing to let each other be; as we are; two diametrically opposite human beings in many ways, which has often led to storminess. But I think we are both learning not to chafe at the other's particular *is*ness. This is the best reason I can think of why ontology is my word for the summer.

A Russian priest, Father Anthony, told me, "To say to anyone 'I love you' is tantamount to saying 'You shall live forever.' "

I am slowly beginning to learn something about immortality.

Our children are hungry for words like Father Anthony's. They have a passionate need for the dimension of transcendence, mysticism, way-outness. We're not offering it to them legitimately. The tendency of the churches to be relevant and more-secular-than-thou does not answer our need for the transcendent. As George Tyrrell wrote about a hundred years ago, "If [man's] craving for the mysterious, the wonderful, the supernatural, be not fed on true religion, it will feed itself on the garbage of any superstition that is offered to it."

Hence the interest in mind-expanding drugs, in black magic, occultism, and a kind of superficial Buddhism or Hinduism, as though these totally demanding disciplines could be mastered overnight. And everybody, it seems, is looking to the stars, towards astrology and the occult in general. A friend and I recently had a talk which clarified a few things for me. He told me about going into a Doubleday bookstore and seeing, over the section marked RELIGION, a handwritten card: OCCULT. When he next went to that bookstore, RELIGION was gone: OCCULT was in.

I started going on in high philosophical vein about what a snare and a delusion this is, and could see that he thought I wasn't being very bright.

Suddenly I said, "Hey, I think I know why astrology has such tremendous appeal. The year and month and day you are born matters. The very moment you are born matters. This gives people a sense of their own value as persons that the church hasn't been giving them."

"Now," he said, "you're cooking with gas."

To matter in the scheme of the cosmos: this is better theology than all our sociology. It is, in fact, all that God has promised to us: that we matter. That he cares. As far as I know, no great prophet has promised people that God will give them social justice, though he may have threatened doom and extinction if the people themselves don't do something about it. If God cares about us, we have to care about each other.

Sociology is rational. God is not.

God knows the very moment we are born.

.. 9 ..

We often respond to the rejection and contempt of youth towards parents by such thoughts as: Why would my child feel or act this way? I've always given him everything he wants. I've made do with less just so he could have a good allowance and all the clothes and cars he wants. I haven't made harsh rules; he can stay out as late as he likes, and I never question who he's with. And this is the thanks I get.

Happily, more and more of us are coming to realize that such a parent is an ogre to the under-thirties. This kind of parent has given the child all the material goods of the world and not enough of the structured and disciplined love that would make the child truly free. Such a parent has earned, instead of the respect and admiration he was trying to buy, nothing but distrust and contempt. He is the "ugly adult" the child does not want to become.

What about the mothers who loathe the thought of getting old, who think it a disgrace to look or act their age, as though becoming mature were something to be ashamed of instead of rejoiced in, mothers who pride themselves on dressing like their teenage daughters, and consider it a compliment when people say they look like sisters. Perhaps the daughter doesn't want a sister; perhaps she wants a mother. Here I am grateful for my resemblance to the giraffe—this is one temptation not available to me. On the rare occasions when someone, thinking to flatter and please, has made the "more like a sister than her mother" remark, my reaction has been rejection. I'd far rather be a reasonable-looking fifty-one than a raddled thirty.

And what about the men who make a fetish of being hearty pals to their sons? What sixteen-year-old boy wants a forty-year-old man as a pal? I'm not talking about friendship; that's something else again. Maybe he'd rather have a father instead, a father who, with love, says, You may go this far and no further, a father who makes rules and sets limits, who, when he says no, means no. Friendship, regardless of chronology, is based on mutual respect.

There's enough French in my blood for me to agree with the European attitude that the very young can be charming and delightful and pretty but only a mature woman can be beautiful; and only a mature man can be strong enough to be truly tender.

Jung disagreed with Freud that the decisive period in our lives is the first years. Instead, Jung felt that the decisive period is that in which my husband and I are now, the period of our middle years, when we have passed through childhood with its dependency on our parents; when we've weathered the storms of adolescence and the first probings into the ultimate questions; when we've gone through early adulthood with its problems of career and marriage and bringing up our babies; and for the first time in our lives find ourselves alone before the crucial problem of who, after all these years, we are. All the protective covering of the first three stages is gone, and we are suddenly alone with ourselves and have to look directly at the great and unique problem of the meaning of our own particular existence in this particular universe.

The breakup of many marriages at precisely this point is another symptom of our refusal to accept this vitally important period of our lives. We have—particularly in the United States, particularly in the suburbs—allowed ourselves to live in a child-centered world; the children have become more important to the parents than the parents are to each other; and suddenly the children grow up and leave the nest and the parents find themselves alone with each other, and discover with horror that there is nobody there. Their youth is gone, and they haven't become anybody, least of all themselves, and in their terror they have to escape from themselves even further.

So we extol the virtue of chronological, rather than actual, youth. Our younger daughter amused us highly several years ago at the dinner table by looking at us and saying, "Well, really, Mother and Daddy, you're finished. I mean, it's all ahead of us, but you've had it." She could not understand what we found so hilarious.

One of our children came to us as a legacy from her parents, close friends of ours who died within a year of each other, leaving a seven-year-old daughter. These two deaths, sudden, unexpected, must have seemed to the little girl like total betrayal. "Not her Mommy!" one of her friends cried. To the small child Mommy is still god, and therefore immortal, and must not betray the child and the universe by dying.

For various legal reasons, Maria was not allowed to come to us for several months after her mother's death, and this period of being homeless, without family, was wholly destructive, adding to the loss and upheaval. Her quite natural response was to test the cosmos: if there is any structure or reason to life, prove it. She broke rules, because only thus could she have it shown to her that there are rules. It was my husband who came up with the one punishment which had any effect when she got completely out of hand: we took away all rules. You don't want to go to bed at bedtime? Stay up as late as you like. It's your turn to set the table? Forget it. You don't want to wear the dress Mother's put out for you? Wear whatever you like. You enjoy living in a pigpen? Fine, don't tidy your room.

This was the one thing she could not stand, to have us remove the security of loving discipline. It wasn't more than a short while before we would find her stealing into the dining room to set the table.

Possibly one of the reasons so many of us have relinquished our proper roles as parents is a reaction to the warning of Zeke's psychiatrist from Omaha: we are so afraid of manipulating, of taking away essential freedom and replacing it with imprisoning structures, that we withdraw. Added to this, the widespread misunderstanding of psychiatrists' warnings about the prevalent abuses of parenthood intimidates us. We read about the mother forcing her son to be dependent on her, so that, psychologically, she emasculates him; he becomes incapable of love and blunders into the grey world of narcissism. The father, we are told, forces his superego on his son, thereby diminishing his free will and his capacity to become a man in his own right. And of course there's the old bugaboo of the Oedipus complex, the boy "wanting" his mother and ending up looking for a "girl just like the girl who married dear old Dad." And the girl "falling in love" with her father at puberty and looking for a father, rather than a lover, in her husband.

We swallow half truths without understanding the very real and important truths behind these mythical analogies, and in our terror of becoming destructive mothers and fathers, we refuse to be parents at all. We abdicate parenthood and turn over our responsibilities to strangers; the Sunday School teacher will teach morality (while we brag at the dinner table of "getting around" the government on our income tax); the biology teacher will give sex guidance (it's too embarrassing); the comics and the villains on TV will take care of leisure time and keep the children out of our hair and, what is worse, teach them passivity. If the kids are opting out, we have opted out first.

Sometimes Hugh and I feel that if we have done anything right with our children it has been an accident and a miracle; often we realize, in retrospect, that the things we thought were best weren't really very good at all. Perhaps our children have taught themselves more on our mistakes than on our good will. But we still have to have the courage to make decisions, to say yes, here; no, there.

And there are compensations, lovely unexpected surprises. For instance, one night at dinner after the children's school report cards had arrived in the morning, Maria said, "Mother and Daddy, we really appreciate the way you talked about all the good things on our report cards and didn't yell at us about the bad." (She had had a D in math: so did I, during my school days, far too often.) She went on, "You've no idea how awful most of the kids' parents are; they hit them and yell at them and never even notice if they get a good grade in something." And to our amazement she repeated, "We really do appreciate you."

So, by a happy accident, we had done something right!

.. 10 ..

Something very wrong that our generation, as a whole, has done is to set one example for our children that may be more telling than we realize: we respect old age even less than they do. Our parents, as they grow old, are frequently shuffled off into homes or institutions. We persuade ourselves that they'll be happier there, they'll be better off with their "own kind" (chronological segregation seems to me one of the worst sins of all), but actually the real problem is that we have neither the time nor the space for them in this urban, technological world. I don't speak out of any righteous isolation and I know of no easy solution. My grandfather lived to be one hundred and one. For ninety-five years he was a vital, brilliant human being. At ninety-five he retired—up until his ninety-fifth birthday he went to work every day. When he stopped work, the rest of him began stopping, too. In the end he was little more than a child, and things were—to say the least—not easy. He was not put in an old people's home—our modern equivalent of Bedlam— because my mother took care of him. But, for many people, Bedlam is the only solution. My own mother is now ninety, and not well. I know how I hope to meet the problems which will inevitably arise, but I am not sure that I will be able to.

As for me, when my time comes, I'd like to be put out on an ice floe.

I heard a doctor say that the living tend to withdraw emotionally from the dying, thereby driving them deeper into isolation. Not to withdraw takes tremendous strength. To pull back is a temptation; it doesn't hurt nearly as much as remaining open. But I saw a horrendous example of a family withdrawing from a long death and this, if anything, will keep me from it.

A friend of mine, a writer, only a few years older than I, got cancer of the lungs which almost immediately spread to the brain, giving the effect of a stroke that paralyzed one side. She was put in hospital where she was given powerful radiation treatment which gave her radiation sickness; she looked like a victim of Hiroshima; her hair came out until there were only a few wisps left. She lost weight massively. She lay there in her hospital bed, able to move one hand, to mumble a few words, looking like an ancient mummy. Within this terrifying travesty of a human body she was trapped; she was. I went fairly often, with two of her friends, to see her. At first when we talked to her she could mumble that she was glad to see us. Later on she could no longer speak, but she was still there; she still was. Somewhere the essential being of the bush still lived beneath the burning. If I held her hand she could respond with a pressure. For quite a long while she had strength enough to take my hand, to put it to her lips, her fearful, dried, dying lips, and cover it with little loving kisses. After a while all she could do was to let me know with her fingers against mine that she was still there, that the touch of a hand could still reach her.

Her husband and her two children, both college age, had stopped going to see her. It was too painful for them. It is dangerous to judge; but I judged. I was only a friend; she needed her family and they were abandoning her; they had completely withdrawn emotionally. She was, as far as they were concerned, already dead.

But she wasn't dead. She was there, and she needed to be touched. The essential part of her which could not be consumed needed to be recognized. It wasn't that difficult for me and the other two friends to go to her. She was not our mother, child, wife. Our lives would be basically unchanged by her death, except in the sense that our lives are changed by every death. And I think that we all, except perhaps nurses and doctors who see it all the time, have a primitive instinct to withdraw from death, even if we manage to conceal our pulling away. There is always the *memento mori*, the realization that death is contagious; it is contracted the moment we are conceived.

I always took a bath when I got home from the hospital.

It takes a tremendous maturity, a maturity I don't possess, to strike the balance of involvement/detachment which makes us creatively useful, able to be compassionate, to be involved in the other person's suffering rather than in our own response to it. False compassion, or sentimentality, always leads us to escape by withdrawing, by becoming cold and impassive and wounding.

As modern medicine keeps people alive far beyond the old threescore years and ten, the problem increases. Evading a realistic acceptance of death and old age hurts not only our parents but our children, and even when it *is* accepted responsibly, it is criticized. Friends of ours in New York are being censured because the wife's father is dying in their apartment: he should be put in a hospital, they are told; how can you let your children see death?

But this old man does not require specialized nursing; he does require love and acceptance, and he can have this in his own family in a way in which it can never be given even in the best of hospitals. Which children are being shown the true example of mature love? Those who are asked to share life and death? Or those who are "spared" all unpleasantness? Which children are being helped to become redeemed adults?

And here I come to a dichotomy in my thinking as far as my own children are concerned. I cannot bear the thought of being a burden to them, of becoming senile and silly and an exacerbation. I would be willing—I hope—to accept such a burden myself, but I never want to *be* one. There is something more than pride involved here. We've taken a wrong turning somewhere, so long ago, that we no longer know what is the right way.

I was deeply involved in the deaths of both my grandmothers. I was affected and perhaps scarred, but I think the scarring came more from misguided attempts on the part of varied adults to push me aside, keep things secret, protect me from what I already knew, than from my parents allowing me to share in both life and death.

After my maternal grandmother's death I was taken to the funeral, but not to the cemetery. I remember being in the house with my grandmother's dog, who showed his loss by retreating under the bed in which she had died, and refusing to move. I sat alone in my small bedroom and the sea wind blew and the waves rolled slowly, unremittingly, in to shore, and my own grief and incomprehension of death became too much for me to bear. So I picked up a book, a book I had already read and loved, and moved out of my own world of numb pain and into the world of the book. I do not think that this was escape or evasion. The heroine of the book had her own problems with loneliness and anxiety and death. Sharing these, being totally in this different world for an hour or so, helped me understand my own feelings.

.. 11 ..

After a day spent in the emergency room of a city hospital, a day in which I was surrounded by accidents, dying children, irritable patients, many of whom spoke no English and could not follow directions, incredible patience on the part of under-staffed doctors and nurses, I felt somewhat the same sense of irrationality in the world around me (all these people were there by accident) as did the man who was almost killed by the falling beam. Whenever this occurs I turn to the piano, to my typewriter, to a book. We turn to stories and pictures and music because they show us who and what and why we are, and what our relationship is to life and death, what is essential, and what, despite the arbitrariness of falling beams, will not burn. Paul Klee said, "Art does not reproduce the visible. Rather, it makes visible." It is not then, at its best, a mirror but an icon. It takes the chaos in which we live and shows us structure and pattern, not the structure of conformity which imprisons but the structure which liberates, sets us free to become growing, mature human beings. We are a generation which is crying loudly to tear down all structure in order to find freedom, and discovering, when order is demolished, that instead of freedom we have death.

A year ago I taught a seminar in writing practices at the General Theological Seminary in Chelsea. One evening I walked in and announced, "Tonight we are going to talk about structure," well aware that I was stirring up a hornet's nest. One cannot talk about structure in literature without talking about it in all of life, and structure, that year, was out. But I wanted to show structure not as restrictive, pharisaic law but as the means of freedom.

We started out discussing the structure of some of the great novels and plays, and went on to structure in poetry, moving from the rhythmic structure of "free" verse to the incredible obedience to structure demanded in the sonnet. The sonnet, as I discovered during the writing of *Wrinkle*, is for me the perfect analogy of the structure which liberates. Meg is to return to the evil planet, Camazotz, in a final attempt to free her little brother from the grip of the rigid structure which imprisons. Mrs Whatsit, one of the extraterrestrial beings who befriend her, says,

"I cannot pretend that we are doing anything but sending you into the gravest kind of danger. I have to acknowledge quite openly that it may be a fatal danger. I know this. But I do not believe it. And the Happy Medium doesn't believe it, either."

"Can't she see what's going to happen?" Calvin asked.

"Oh, not in this kind of thing." Mrs Whatsit sounded surprised at his question. "If we knew ahead of time what was going to happen, we'd be—we'd be like the people in Camazotz, with no lives of our own, with everything all planned and done for us. How can I explain it to you? Oh, I know. In your language you have a form of poetry called the sonnet."

"Yes, yes," Calvin said impatiently. "What's that got to do with the Happy Medium?"

"Kindly pay me the courtesy of listening to me." Mrs Whatsit's voice was stern, and for a moment Calvin stopped pawing the ground like a nervous colt. "It is a very strict form of poetry, is it not?"

"Yes."

"There are fourteen lines, I believe, all in iambic pentameter. That's a very strict rhythm or meter, yes?"

"Yes." Calvin nodded.

"And each line has to end with a precise rhyme pattern. And if the poet does not do it exactly this way, it is not a sonnet, is it?"

"No."

"But within this strict form the poet has complete freedom to say whatever he wants, doesn't he?"

"Yes." Calvin nodded again.

"So," Mrs Whatsit said.

"So what?"

"Oh, do not be stupid, boy!" Mrs Whatsit scolded. "You know perfectly well what I am driving at!"

"You mean you're comparing our lives to a sonnet? A strict form, but freedom within it?"

"Yes," Mrs Whatsit said. "You're given the form, but you have to write the sonnet yourself. What you say is completely up to you."

Well, there it is: an analogy.

To speak analogously is to admit that you can't say it directly; you really can't say it at all; it's outside the realm of provable fact. But it is not a coincidence that some of the greatest poetry in the English language is in the form of the sonnet. The haiku is one of the most popular forms of poetry today: what could be more structured?

But the students talked loudly about wanting to be free to dance, to make love, to be themselves. So do I. So we left literature and talked about the body, and I kept asking questions: what is it in you which gives you this freedom? Finally one of the young men, with great reluctance, pulled out the word: skeleton. It is our bones, our structure, which frees us to dance, to make love. Without our structure we would be an imprisoned, amorphous blob of flesh, incapable of response. The amoeba has a minimum of structure, but I doubt if it has much fun.

.. 12 ..

This time in Crosswicks is a respite, perhaps an irresponsible one. For this brief time I am more aware of a baby learning a new word, of the splashing of the brook after a rain, of the is-ness of lying in our big four-poster bed on a night when I retire with the babies and watch the green fade from the trees which surround our windows. But I am very much aware that what we are all, in our country and around the world, going to do in the next weeks and months and years is of inestimable importance. In the past few years we have seen more violence and horror than we would have thought possible, and there aren't any signs that it is going to stop without a great deal of pain and anguish.

Thomas Mann wrote that if the German writers had, through their fiction, made richer promises than Hitler, it would have been Hitler, rather than the writers, who would have had to flee the country. The idea of this kind of responsibility hit me a lot harder than the idea of being an orally regressed psychic masochist.

I am naïve again, perhaps, in thinking that the love and laughter of Crosswicks is, in its own way, the kind of responsibility Mann was talking about. I do not think that it is naïve to think that it is the tiny, particular acts of love and joy which are going to swing the balance, rather than general, impersonal charities. These acts are spontaneous, unself-conscious, realized only late if at all. They may be as quiet as pulling a blanket up over a sleeping baby. Or as noisy as the night of trumpets and stars.

One Saturday this summer was the occasion of the annual Firemen's Rally. They came down the lane in their red fire trucks, around our corner and down the lane to the fairgrounds; they came from four states, and seven counties in Connecticut, and Great-grandmother had a splendid time sitting out on the lawn watching them. In the evening after the rally there was a carnival, and Dana and Margie, two of our summer "children," went with Hugh, coming home with enormous trumpets, like the ones used to announce the arrival of kings in color movie spectaculars—except that these are plastic. But they make a glorious wild bray which sounds like the trumpeting of an elephant. Sunday evening was clear and luminous so we went to the star-watching rock and welcomed the arrival of each star with a blast of trumpet. We lay there, in an odd assortment of coats; I had on an embroidered coat a friend had bought in Dubrovnik; the two girls had on ancient fur coats; and we were covered with blankets. We needed them, even though the rock itself still held the warmth of the sun, our own star, and radiated a gentle heat to us as we lay there and watched the sky, blowing the trumpets and sharing a can of insect repellent and listening to the crickets and the katydids and trying to identify the other night singers, and then outsinging them with all the nursery rhymes and songs and hymns we could think of which had stars and alleluias in them.

And I was totally back in joy. I didn't realize I had been out of it, caught in small problems and disappointments and frustrations, until it came surging back. It was as radiant as the rock, and I lay there, listening to the girls trumpeting, and occasionally being handed one of the trumpets so that I could make a loud blast myself, and I half expected to hear a herd of elephants come thundering across the far pastures in answer to our call.

And joy is always a promise.

THREE

One day this past spring a young man who works part-time for the Cathedral came into the library to let off steam. He is not a Christian, and he hates the church in any structured form—what is sometimes called the Establishment. (I war against the Establishment, too, but I want it to be there for me to hit at.) He began judgmentally denouncing all the clergy for being hypocrites.

"Wait a minute," I said. "Just what do you mean by hypocrite?"

They did not, it seemed, live up to his standard for clergymen. I was willing to concede that not only was this undoubtedly true but they probably didn't live up to their own standards for clergymen, either. Trying not to be equally judgmental, because everything I said to him hit my own weaknesses, I said, "You talk a lot about your integrity, but you go on working here, taking every advantage the Cathedral gives you, and disapproving vocally of everything it stands for. How do you manage that? How close is the 'you' of your ideals to the 'you' of reality? When I react the way you've just been doing about someone else's behavior, it usually stops me short if I remember how far my actual self is from the self I would like to be."

One of the reasons this young man and I are friends is not so much that he is willing to stand there and let me pontificate but that he understands what I'm getting at. "You mean," he said slowly, "that what I'm really doing, underneath, is talking about myself?"

"Yes, but not only you. All of us. We all do it."

The most "whole" people I know are those in whom the gap between the "ontological" self and the daily self is the smallest. The Latin *integer* means untouched; intact. In mathematics, an integer is a whole number. The people I know who are intact don't have to worry about their integrity; they are incapable of doing anything which would break it.

It's a sad commentary on our world that "integrity" has slowly been coming to mean self-centeredness. Most people who worry about their integrity are thinking about it in terms of themselves. It's a great excuse for not doing something you really don't want to do, or are afraid to do: "I can't do that and keep my integrity." Integrity, like humility, is a quality which vanishes the moment we are conscious of it in ourselves. We see it only in others.

The gap between our "real" and "actual" selves is, to some degree, in all of us; no one is completely whole. It's part of what makes us human beings instead of gods. It's part of our heritage from our mythical forebears, from Adam and Eve. When we refuse to face this gap in ourselves, we widen it.

It is only a sacramental view of life which helps me to understand and bear this gap; it is only my "icons," which, lovingly and laughingly, point it out to me: not only the Buddha; throughout the years others have come to help me.

People like Una, as well as Buddhas, can be icons for me. Una feels, with justification, that she has been betrayed by the Establishment. One of these betrayals came when she went to church and was made to feel unwelcome because she was black. Una is for revolution. And so, I discover, am I.

What is the Establishment? What is revolution?

They are not incompatible. Each is essential to the life of the other. If they are to live at all, they must live symbiotically, each taking nourishment from the other, each giving nourishment in return. The Establishment is not, thank God, the Pentagon, or corruption in the White House or governors' palaces or small-town halls. It is not church buildings of any denomination. It is not organized groups, political parties, hierarchies, synods, councils, or whatever. It is simply the company of people who acknowledge that we cannot live in isolation, or by our own virtue, but need community and mystery, expressed in the small family, and then the larger families of village, church, city, country, globe.

Because we are human, these communities tend to become rigid. They stop evolving, revolving, which is essential to their life, as is the revolution of the earth about the sun essential to the life of our planet, our full family and basic establishment. Hence, we must constantly be in a state of revolution, or we die. But revolution does not mean that the earth flings away from the sun into structureless chaos. As I understand the beauty of the earth's dance around the sun, so also do I understand the constant revolution of the community of the Son.

But we forget, and our revolutions run down and die, like a record on an old, windup phonograph.

My own forgetfulness, the gap between the real, revolutionary me and the less alive creature who pulls me back, is usually only too apparent. But my husband and I have been encouraged by the fact that we ourselves have learned something about love and honor and loyalty as we have tried to teach these values to our children. And I have learned from the very stories I write. This is a humbling process, but also a joyful one.

So my hope, each day as I grow older, is that this will never be simply chronological aging—which is a nuisance and frequently a bore—the old 'bod' at over half a century has had hard use; it won't take what it did a few years ago—but that I will also grow into maturity, where the experience which can be acquired only through chronology will teach me how to be more aware, open, unafraid to be vulnerable, involved, committed, to accept disagreement without feeling threatened (repeat and underline this one), to understand that I cannot take myself seriously until I stop taking myself seriously—to be, in fact, a true adult.

To be.

. . 2 . .

The focus of our days is the dinner table, whether, as often happens in the winter nowadays, it is just Hugh and me or I am cooking for a dozen or more. When the children were in school I didn't care what time we ate dinner as long as we ate it together. If Hugh were going to be late, then we would all be late. If he had to be at the theatre early, we would eat early. This was the time the community (except for the very small babies) gathered together, when I saw most clearly illustrated the beautiful principle of unity in diversity: we were one, but we were certainly diverse, a living example of the fact that like and equal are not the same thing.

While Alan was teaching and finishing his master's degree, he ate a good many meals with us, for he often had to be in our neighborhood. Somehow it often happens at our table that we get into great and lovely battles (Alan and I seldom *fight*; when we do we are like two five-year-olds, and neither of us can bear it until we have made up). My usual battles with him are lovely because we are basically on the same side; they are nevertheless battles. Sometimes my husband acts as devil's advocate; he's very good at it. Sometimes the adversary is the darkness that roams the earth. During one dinner, Alan mentioned the men who feel that it is not God who is dead, as some theologians were then saying, but language that is dead. If language is to be revived or, like the phoenix, born of its own ashes, then violence must be done to it.

This seemed to me to be a distinct threat. If language is dead, so is my profession. How can one write books in a dead language? And what did he mean by "doing violence to language"? I began to argue heatedly, and in the midst of my own argument I began to see that doing violence to language means precisely the opposite of what I thought it meant. To do violence to language, in the sense in which he used the phrase, is not to use long words, or strange orders of words, or even to do anything unusual at all with the words in which we attempt to communicate. It means really speaking to each other, destroying platitudes and jargon and all the safe cushions of small talk with which we insulate ourselves; not being afraid to talk about the things we don't talk about, the ultimate things that really matter. It means turning again to the words that affirm meaning, reason, unity, that teach responsible rather than selfish love. And sometimes, doing violence to language means not using it at all, not being afraid of being silent together, of being silent alone. Then, through the thunderous silence, we may be able to hear a still, small voice, and words will be born anew.

Tallis says that the greatest music ever written is the silence between the Crucifixus and the Resurrexus est in Bach's Mass in B minor. Yes; and I would add that some of the greatest writing mankind has ever produced comes in the caesura; the pause between words.

Why are we so afraid of silence? Teenagers cannot study without their records; they walk along the street with their transistors. Grownups are as bad if not worse; we turn on the TV or the radio the minute we come into the house or start the car. The pollution of noise in our cities is as destructive as the pollution of air. We show our fear of silence in our conversation: I wonder if the orally-minded Elizabethans used "um" and "er" the way we do? And increasingly prevalent is what my husband calls an articulated pause: "You know." We interject "you know" meaninglessly into every sentence, in order that the flow of our speech should not be interrupted by such a terrifying thing as silence.

If I look to myself I find, as usual, contradiction. Ever since I've had a record player I've written to music—not all music, mostly Bach and Mozart and Scarlatti and people like that—but music: sound.

Yet when I went on my first retreat I slipped into silence as though into the cool waters of the sea. I felt totally, completely, easily at home in silence.

With the people I love most I can sit in silence indefinitely.

We need both for our full development; the joy of the sense of sound; and the equally great joy of its absence.

. . 3 . .

Our youngest child, when he first became conscious of vocabulary, often did violence to words in absurd little ways which delighted us. Hugh and I listened seriously, lest we make him self-conscious, or think we were laughing at him. We needn't have worried; he plunged into vocabulary like a sea gull into water, entirely fascinated with whatever he came up with. Even the laughter of his elder siblings did not deter him, and he is now happily malaproping in Latin, French, and German. One day, aged seven, he came home from school highly indignant because the boys' gym period had been curtailed. "We only had ten minutes of gym," he said, "and that was all anesthetics."

This was not just something to laugh at; it sent me back to my own, dreaded gym periods where anesthetics rather than calisthenics would have been more than welcome. Any team I was on lost automatically; when teams were chosen, mine was the last name to be reluctantly called out, and the team which had the bad luck to get me let out uninhibited groans. I now have this emotion at my fingertips if I need it for a story I'm writing; or if I need it to comfort some child who is going through a similar experience. It does us good to listen to things differently.

I remember "anesthetics" not only because it reminded me of my own pains over gym but because this small, delectable laugh came while I was in the middle of a very bad period, literarily speaking, and needed any reason for laughter, no matter how trivial. *A Wrinkle in Time* was on its long search for a publisher. Finally one, who had kept the manuscript for three months, turned it down on the Monday before Christmas. I remember sitting on the foot of our bed, tying up Christmas presents, and feeling cold and numb: anesthetized. I was congratulating myself on being controlled and grownup, and found out only later that I'd made a mess of the Christmas presents; I'd sent some heady perfume to a confirmed bachelor, and a sober necktie to a sixteen-year-old girl. So I called Theron, my agent: "Send the manuscript back to me. Nobody's ever going to take it, it's too peculiar, and it just isn't fair to the family." He didn't want to send it back, but I was cold and stubborn, and finally he gave in.

My mother was with us for the holidays, and shortly after Christmas I had a small party for her with some of her old friends. One of them, Hester Stover, more than ever dear to me now, said, "Madeleine, you must meet my friend, John Farrar." I made some kind of disgruntled noise, because I never wanted to see another publisher; I was back to thinking I ought to learn to bake cherry pie. But Hester, going to a good deal of trouble, insisted on setting up an appointment, and I took the subway down to John Farrar's office. I just happened to have that rather bulky manuscript under my arm.

He couldn't have been kinder or warmer. He knew some of my other work and was generous enough to say that he liked it, and he asked me what I was up to now. I explained that I had a book that I kind of liked, but nobody else did, or if they did, they were afraid of it.

I left it with him. Within two weeks I was having lunch with him and Hal Vursell, and signing a contract. "But don't be disappointed if it doesn't do well," they told me. "We're publishing it because we love it."

It is a right and proper Cinderella story. And I'm sure Cinderella appreciated her ball gown more because she'd been forced to sit by the ashes in rags for a long time before her fairy godmother arrived. There's another moral to the fairy tale, too: the golden coach can very easily turn back into a pumpkin.

And here's where I must stretch the image a little further: glass slippers went with the ball gown and the golden coach, and glass slippers are fragile things. If one's feet grow too big, the slippers break; if one stamps around instead of dancing in them, they shatter.

Both children and adults ask me: "What did you do when you heard that *A Wrinkle in Time* had won the Newbery Medal?"

It's an easy question to answer, because it's a moment I couldn't possibly forget. It was in the morning, just as I was hurrying the children off to school. My husband, who was in a play on Broadway, was asleep, and if there's an unbreakable rule in our household, it is that we do not wake Daddy up in the morning, and we don't speak to him until after he's had two cups of coffee, read the paper, and done his crossword puzzle.

The telephone rang. It was long distance, and an impossible connection. I couldn't hear anything. The operator told me to hang up and she'd try again. The long-distance phone ringing unexpectedly always makes me nervous: is something wrong with one of the grandparents? The phone rang again, and still the connection was full of static and roaring, so the operator told me to hang up and she'd try once more. This time I could barely hear a voice: "This is Ruth Gagliardo, of the Newbery-Caldecott committee." There was a pause, and she asked, "Can you hear me?" "Yes, I can hear you." Then she told me that *Wrinkle* had won the medal. My response was an inarticulate squawk; Ruth told me later that it was a special pleasure to her to have me *that* excited.

We hung up, and I flew through the dining room and the living room like a winged giraffe, burst open the bedroom door, flew in, gave a great leap, and landed on the bed on top of my startled husband.

Joy!

Farrar, Straus and Giroux have now published ten of my books, and I hope we will be bedfellows forever. They are generous with me in all kinds of ways, and I appreciate especially that they will let me try many different forms of writing. One of the reasons I went unhappily from publishing house to publishing house before F S & G took me on was that I would write a book, it would have a moderate success, and then the publisher would want me to do another book like it: you've done it in pink, dear, now do it in blue. But I'd write something quite different, and there I was, out in the cold again. My friends at Farrar, Straus and Giroux allow me to experiment, which is the only way a writer grows.

After the unexpected success of *Wrinkle* I was invited to quite a lot of literary bashes, and frequently was approached by publishers who had rejected *Wrinkle*. "I wish you had sent the book to us." I usually could respond, "But I did." One publisher absolutely refused to believe that his house had rejected the book, and I had to go to my journal and show him the page where I had recorded my misery on the day that his house had said no. "But *I* never saw it," he cried. "It never got to me."

There's a reason for this, chaps—though, like Alan's chemistry master, I'm not sure what it is. No senior editor could possibly read all the manuscripts that come across his desk. A manuscript by an unknown writer obviously must be read first by someone with less experience than the senior editor's, and there seems to be no solution to that problem. Editors are aware that good books are rejected because of this. Even a published writer is often read by the most junior of readers; *Wrinkle* was my seventh book. In about half the houses to which it was sent it was given the dignity of being read by one of the senior editors; in the other half it was not. And it is, I suppose, an odd book.

When Hal Vursell was asked why they had accepted it when other publishers were afraid of it, he replied, both privately and publicly in a published article from which I quote briefly: "We have all, from time to time, chosen and published obviously superior books, a book not written to prescription or formula, one which we passionately believed to be far better than nine-tenths of what was currently being offered, only to have that very book still-born. Now editors have emotions, too, and when this happens, believe it or not, they bleed. All of us have a longer or shorter list of such books we still mourn. But if this happens to an editor too often, he loses his ability to judge and dare creatively; he has a strong urge to retreat permanently to the sluggish waters of 'safe' publishing. So to have refused *A Wrinkle in Time* carries no stigma of editorial cowardice; the bravest of us pause from time to time to bind up our wounds. It was our own good fortune that the manuscript reached us at a moment when we were ready to do battle again."

It was my good fortune, too.

But one must not take good fortune too seriously. A librarian told me, with anxiety on my behalf, that she had known authors who, after winning such an award, were unable to write again; it produced such self-consciousness that the result was writer's block. I was able to assure her that I was deep in the middle of another book, and that when I am writing I think of nothing but the book. Success or failure matters to me—and matters too much—*after* the book is written. I know what the book wanted to be, for each book has its own ontology; but have I managed, in revision after revision, to catch enough of the essential book that cried out to me to write it? I am never sure.

Strange: if a review is good, I am delighted, but I don't take it quite seriously. If a review is bad, I fall right into that old trap of hurt pride: hubris.

During the writing, however, there is nothing but the book itself.

During the ten years when practically nothing I wrote was published, I was as much writer qua writer as I am now; it may happen that there will come another time when I can't find anyone to publish my work. If this happens it will matter. It will hurt. But I did learn, on that fortieth birthday, that success is not my motivation.

I am grateful for that terrible birthday, which helps me to wear glass slippers lightly, very lightly. My laughing white china Buddha helps, too. He is barefooted.

. . 4 . .

One unexpected and joyful result of the Newbery Medal has been friends. I can't possibly name them all; if I mention A. I can't leave out B., and then there's C., and on down through the whole alphabet. They have come to me, these warm and generous people, through talks across the country: a few minutes' conversation, real talk, with somebody will lead to a correspondence out of which a deep friendship will grow. It just happens that several people have spoken lately about how we must learn not to *need* anybody; I know that I need my friends. All of them, even those I seldom see.

I enjoy trekking about the country to give talks: I don't do too many—my job is to write, not lecture, and it is also to stay home with my family and do the cooking. But I do love my occasional jaunts, although my hands still get cold with nervousness before I speak. It is not good to be too nervous, but I think it is essential to be a little nervous; one ought to care that much. My husband tells me that no matter how long a play has been running, he feels the same kind of nervousness every night before he goes on stage. It may be partly pride, but I think that it's mostly the desire to do a good job, not for one's own satisfaction, but for the sake of the job itself. It's part of what

Zeke and I talked about this July, and why I always say that psalm verse before starting.

I also enjoy being on panels, either with grownups or with teenagers. One day Hal Vursell called me, after having made arrangements for me to be on a radio program where six youngsters from schools all over New York talk to a writer about his book. I'd been on this particular program several times before, and always enjoyed it, even if the kids pull no punches. If they don't like something they say so. I learn, probably, more from what they don't like than from their unqualified appreciation.

Hal said, "Now I have something to tell you that I think will please you. Miss X said, 'We do like to have Miss L'Engle on this program. Lots of people become very prima donna-ish when they've had as much success as she has, but it hasn't affected her at all.' "

Hasn't it?

Of course it has. It's made me free to go out to meet people without tangling in the pride which is an inevitable part of the sense of failure. W. Somerset Maugham said, "The common idea that success spoils people by making them vain, egotistic and self-complacent is erroneous; on the contrary, it makes them, for the most part, humble, tolerant, and kind. Failure makes people bitter and cruel."

I recorded this rather bitterly in my journal during the time of failure. It's true. My very small success has had a joyfully liberating effect; so has passing the half-century mark and being happily married; I am free to reach out and touch people without being misunderstood.

5

When I talk with teachers ("in-depth" talking, I think the current jargon would have it) about teaching and the effect that teachers have on the lives of children I tell about two very different teachers I encountered in my early years in New York.

I spent three years when I was very young in a school which was, as far as I was concerned, a foretaste of hell. It was a private school with a fine reputation, academically and socially. It was one of the "proper" schools for a New York child to attend. It did not occur to me that I could tell my parents that I was unhappy. I assumed that it was something to be gone through, and that if I was unhappy I had no one but myself to blame.

In a sense, that is undoubtedly true, but it is not wholly true. At least some of it was the school's fault, and my home-room teacher's fault in particular.

A lot of emphasis was put on athletic prowess in that school. I was a poor runner not just because of innate clumsiness but because an illness when I was three had left one leg shorter than the other, and whenever I was tired I limped. Undoubtedly I was too sensitive to the groans and moans of my classmates at gym; I should have been able to shrug it off and laugh; I couldn't. So my unpopularity quickly extended beyond the gym to the rest of the school world. Our teacher, whose name I happily do not remember, accepted my classmates' assessment of me. Not only was Madeleine clumsy; she was dumb. It wasn't long before I stopped doing my homework: what was the use? The teacher always found fault with it, found something to laugh at, always held it up as an example of what not to do. When I went back to our apartment after school I read books of my own choosing, and I wrote stories and poems, painted pictures, played the piano.

Out of the varied humiliations of that school there are two which stand out particularly. One must have happened during the first year there, and it caused me to discover the perfidy of adults. My parents might be rather more Olympian than the parents of most American children—I did not see a great deal of them while I was a child; at night, for instance, they dined at eight, and always in dinner clothes, and I had my supper in the nursery—but they were models of integrity. I could not imagine an adult doing anything that was wrong.

Adults can, and do, and perhaps the earlier we discover it, the better for us. I was about eight, certainly old enough to have forgotten what it is like to wet one's pants. One day in French class I asked to be excused. The French teacher must have been having problems with children wanting to leave the room for other reasons, and using the bathroom as an excuse, because she forbade me to go. I asked her three times, and three times was told, No. When the bell for the end of class rang I bolted from my desk and ran, but I couldn't quite make it, and spent the rest of the afternoon sodden and shamed.

When my mother heard what had happened, she demanded to see the principal. I remember with awful clarity the scene in the principal's office, after the French teacher had been summoned. She said, "But Madeleine never asked to go to the bathroom. If she had only raised her hand, of course I would have excused her."

She was believed. I suppose the principal had to believe the teacher, rather than the child with wet clothes. I was reprimanded gently, told to ask the next time, and not to lie about it afterwards, it really wasn't anything dreadful to make that kind of mistake.

To have an adult lie, and to have another adult not know that it was a lie; to tell the truth myself and not be believed: the earth shook on its foundations.

I wrote about this incident in *Camilla*, and writing about it helped: to take it away from the personal and objectify it made it comprehensible; I found that I had it in me to pity the French teacher and the principal.

The second of the two incidents happened the spring of my last year there—for it made my mother change schools the following year. A poetry contest was announced for the entire lower school; the judge was to be the head of the upper-school English Department. The entries weren't screened by the home-room teachers, otherwise I wouldn't have had a chance of getting anything in.

When I won, there was great sound and fury. My teacher said that Madeleine must have copied the poem; she couldn't possibly have written it; she isn't very bright, you know.

It was an issue big enough for my parents to hear about it. My mother produced the poems and stories I had been writing while I should have been doing homework, and it was finally conceded that Madeleine could have written that poem after all.

I learned a lot about writing in this school—not directly, because I don't think anybody taught me anything academically—but simply from doing it in order to survive. At O.S.U. this July we asked each other: how much pain and rejection and failure and humiliation can a child take? Pain can be a creative teacher, but there is a point where it is totally destructive. The span of endurance varies from child to child; it is never infinite. What would have happened if my parents had not been able to remove me from that particular school where teacher and student alike had me pegged as different and therefore a failure?

I remember quite clearly coming home in the afternoon, putting my school bag down, and thinking, calmly and bitterly, "I am the cripple, the unpopular girl," leaving my book bag where it lay, and writing a story for myself where the heroine was the kind of girl I would have liked to be.

Warning, parents, teachers, friends: once a child starts to think of himself this way, it's almost impossible for the "image" —I think that's the right word here—to be changed. A few weeks ago the girlfriend of one of my ex-students called me long distance, weeping, because they were having problems. We talked for quite a long time, and I made some reference to my own youthful clumsiness in love, and she said in astonishment, "*You* were that way, too! I've always thought of you as being beautiful and wise and strong."

I was considerably more astonished than she. I still tend to think of myself in the mirror set up for me in that one school. I was given a self-image there, and not a self, and a self-image imposed on one in youth is impossible to get rid of entirely, no matter how much love and affirmation one is given later. Even after all these years, my instinctive image of myself is of someone gawky, clumsy, inadequate, stupid, unwanted, unattractive, in the way . . .

A good deal of the time I can laugh about it. Two schools later—an English one—the irritated form mistress snapped, "Madeleine, can't you come into a room without knocking over the furniture?" I couldn't then, and seldom can now. It doesn't bother me as much as it used to. I simply accept my multifarious black-and-blue spots. But there are times when I wish I believed in reincarnation. I would like to live a life as a ballerina.

6

At the school which followed that unfortunate one, I encountered a teacher whose name and face I *do* remember. I was there only a year, because the following summer we went to Europe to live; but a great deal can be accomplished in a year. My home-room teacher was one of five or six great teachers whose influence has helped shape my life. A young woman on her first job, she was the first to see any potential in a shy, gauche child. My mother tells of my bursting into our apartment, calling out joyfully, "Mother, Mother, you ought to scold me for the sin of gluttony!"

"Whatever for?"

"Miss Clapp liked my story so much that she read it out loud to the whole class, and I was so happy I just gloated and gloated."

Miss Clapp was Margaret Clapp, recently retired as president of Wellesley College.

She didn't make me over completely; I never became graceful, or good at gym, or the most popular girl in school. But I did make friends. And I wrote at least as much during that year, while doing my homework as well, as I had written before. I wrote a sequel to the *Odyssey*, with Telemachus as the hero, and painted lurid illustrations, for a class project. I also wrote my first novel. Fortunately it has been lost, but I remember the plot. It had to do with triplets, boys; one was superb at sports; one was superb academically; and the third was superb socially. So they passed themselves off as one young man and, considering their combined talents, they did very well indeed. Then one of them fell in love and wanted to marry, and he had to tell his sweetheart that he was only one-third of himself.

She walked away from him. All was over. I recall the last line, because I still remember how grownup and sophisticated I felt as I wrote it: "He said nothing. What was there to say?"

I wrote poems, too. Looking through some old journals, I came across several. There was one, notable for its arrogance, if nothing else:

We lived on 82nd Street and the Metropolitan Museum was my short cut to Central Park. I wrote:

I go into the museum
and look at all the pictures on the walls.
Instead of feeling my own insignificance
I want to go straight home and paint.

A great painting, or symphony, or play, doesn't diminish us, but enlarges us, and we, too, want to make our own cry of affirmation to the power of creation behind the universe. This surge of creativity has nothing to do with competition, or degree of talent. When I hear a superb pianist, I can't wait to get to my own piano, and I play about as well now as I did when I was ten. A great novel, rather than discouraging me, simply makes me want to write. This response on the part of any artist is the need to make incarnate the new awareness we have been granted through the genius of someone else.

I used the word "arrogant" about those verses. I take it back. I don't think it's arrogance at all. It is beauty crying out for more beauty.

Surely Miss Clapp must have taught me more than I remember. She encouraged me not only to write but to read, giving me books that would stretch my mind and my vocabulary, push me beyond my capacity. There weren't any limited-vocabulary books in those days. I learned vocabulary by coming across new words in my reading for fun (I'm not speaking about textbooks; that's a different matter and I'm not qualified either to criticize or to praise them). I didn't stop to look up the new words; I was far too interested in what I was reading. By the time I'd come across a word in two or three books, the shades of its meaning would automatically come clear, and the word would be added to my vocabulary.

I have a profound conviction that it is most dangerous to tamper with the word. I've been asked why it's wrong to provide the author of a pleasure book, a non-textbook, with a controlled-vocabularly list. First of all, to give an author a list of words and tell him to write a book for children using no word that is not on the list strikes me as blasphemy. What would have happened to Beatrix Potter if she had written in the time of controlled vocabulary? Lettuce has a *soporific* effect on Peter Rabbit. "Come come, Beatrix, that word is beyond a child's vocabulary." "But it's the right word, it's the only possible word." "Nonsense. You can't use soporific because it's outside the child's reading capacity. You can say that lettuce made Peter feel sleepy."

I shudder.

To give a writer a controlled-vocabulary list is manipulating both writer and reader. It keeps the child within his present capacity, on the bland assumption that growth is even and orderly and rational, instead of something that happens in great unexpected leaps and bounds. It ties the author down and takes away his creative freedom, and completely ignores the fact that the good writer will always limit himself. The simplest word is almost always the right word. I am convinced that Beatrix Potter used "soporific" because it was, it really and truly was, the only right word for lettuce at that moment. One of my favorite authors, Anon, wrote, centuries ago:

The written word
Should be clean as bone,
Clear as light,
Firm as stone.
Two words are not
As good as one.

I should pay more attention to those lines than I do. The writer who listens to them will do his own limiting, but it will come from inside, it will come from a creative response and not from an arbitrary restriction, which is the structure that imprisons instead of the structure that liberates.

The more limited our language is, the more limited we are; the more limited the literature we give to our children, the more limited their capacity to respond, and therefore, in their turn, to create. The more our vocabulary is controlled, the less we will be able to think for ourselves. We do think in words, and the fewer words we know, the more restricted our thoughts. As our vocabulary expands, so does our power to think. Try to comprehend an abstract idea without words: we may be able to imagine a turkey dinner. But try something more complicated; try to ask questions, to look for meaning: without words we don't get very far. If we limit and distort language, we limit and distort personality.

Madison Avenue, my old bugaboo, is one of the greatest of all limiters. The more vocabulary is limited, the less people will be able to think for themselves, the more they can be manipulated, and the more of the product they will buy: selling the product is Madison Avenue's end; limiting the public's capacity to think for itself is its means.

"What Madison Avenue wants to do," I said to the students at

O.S.U., deliberately using a violent word for shock value, "is screw the public."

In my excitement—I feel very strongly about this—I used the phrase several times. I found out later at dinner with several of the students and an elderly professor that he was the only one who had even noticed the phrase. He mentioned it at dinner, wondering why I had used it, and the others looked completely baffled.

I explained that I had used it deliberately, because I wanted to emphasize what I was saying, and therefore wanted to use a word which would have shock value. But, except to a man who had passed his seventieth birthday, it hadn't.

Alas. What have we done to our good, bawdy, Anglo-Saxon four-letter words? We have not done violence to them; we have done the opposite. We have blunted them so with overuse that they no longer have any real meaning for us.

"Screw the public," said I, at half a century plus one, and the students, all younger, took it for granted. It had no more impact than if I had said, "Madison Avenue is trying to *do* the public."

When will we be able to redeem our shock words? They have been turned to marshmallows. They need violence done to them again; they need to be wrested from banality; saved for the crucial moment. We no longer have anything to cry in time of crisis.

"Help!" we bleat. And no one hears us. "Help" is another of those four-letter words that don't mean anything any more.

. . 7 . .

It's another of those odd contradictions: we combine controlled vocabulary with totally uncontrolled vocabulary and end up with our language impoverished. It strikes me as somewhat odd that the people who use God's name most frequently, both in life and in literature, usually don't believe in him. Yet their speech and/or writing is liberally sprinkled with "God" and "Jesus" and "Chrissakes." But if I pause and think, it's quite apparent that there's a reason for that . . .

Another contemporary contradiction is that more books are being published today than ever before but educated people are reading less. Over a decade ago I was sent a questionnaire from college; the questionnaire, when collated, would give some idea of what we had done and become since graduation. One of the questions was, "How many books have you read in the past year?"

Most of the girls with whom I went to college were moderately privileged intellectually. Smith has never been an easy college to get into. I felt very ashamed when I answered that particular question, "Two or three books a week."

When the questionnaire was collated there was horror at the answer to that particular question: a high percentage had read no books at all.

All right: our children were little; this is not an age of many servants; most of us had a good deal to struggle with. But *no* books? I read while I'm stirring the white sauce, while I'm in the subway, in the bath.

I don't believe it's coincidence that there was at this same time a great deal of emphasis on controlling not only vocabulary but the content of the books children were to read: no reference to death, to evil, to sex. Not only were new books which mentioned these taboos not being published, but children were no longer given many of the books I grew up on, myths and fairy tales and nursery rhymes. But I have never forgotten the things I learned from Mother Goose, Hans Christian Andersen, and the Brothers Grimm, some of whose stories are admittedly pretty grim.

Consider the grimness of these stories. I read them unexpurgated. My children have my old copy. Some of the stories deal quite openly with evil and sin and death, and the suffering of the innocent while the wicked flourish. The princess doesn't always get the prince. The clever, wicked fellow often triumphs over innocent virtue. Is it or isn't it a good idea to let our children read this kind of story?

I'm like most mothers; my immediate instinct is protective. I tend to be very much a mother lion when it comes to my cubs. But then I remember the eagles, who also love their fledglings. In their great, beautiful nests, protected from all danger by their tremendous height, where no marauder can menace the little ones, the mother and father eagle have carefully woven thorns. These thorns are sharply turned inwards so that the fledglings won't be *too* comfortable.

My husband and I have tried never to make the nest too cozy. And we certainly did not limit our children's reading—or did we? In that paradoxical sense, I suppose yes, we did. My husband, after a hard day's work, enjoys sitting down and relaxing over a Martini before dinner; this is good, this quiet hour of talk and laughter. But we didn't ask our small children to come and share Martinis with us. There is a proper time and a proper place. It's the same with books. We didn't read Faulkner's *Sanctuary* aloud at their bedtime. Nevertheless, we were aware that we had to try to prepare them for the rough world outside the nest. Hans Christian Andersen lets the little match girl die. The Red Queen is pretty rough with Alice, and Lewis Carroll makes no bones about the fact that the sweet little oysters end up by getting eaten. In my mother's old Victorian children's novels, death was often an integral part of the story.

It has been said, and truly said, that reading the Grimms, that weeping for the death of the Selfish Giant, that having witches be bad, and trolls ferocious, leaves its mark on the children. So it does.

When I was little a group of older children terrorized me with games of witches taken from fairy tales. It may—or may not—be because of this that I take the current interest in witchcraft seriously; I do not take evil lightly, or think that it's unimportant and can be coped with easily.

An example of the permanent effect of a book is that of *Charlotte's Web* on our elder daughter. She read it, aged eight, and when she had finished she was in a mood all day, very close to tears because of Charlotte's death at the end. I tried to explain to her that according to the spider calendar Charlotte had lived to be a very old lady, and had had a fine life, lived as long as any spider does, and longer than many. But that only partially comforted her. Then we came to Wilbur the pig.

"Mother," she said, "why did Mr. Zuckerman want to kill Wilbur?"

"Well, Mr. Zuckerman was a farmer, and farmers do kill pigs and sell them for meat."

"Have *we* ever eaten pig?"

"Yes. Often."

"When?"

"Well, whenever we have ham, that's pig. Or bacon. Or pork chops. Or sausage."

"I *hate* sausage!"

Sausage had always been one of her favorite dishes. But to this day she does not care for pig. She denies that Wilbur had anything to do with this, but she has little to say when I inform her that the entire conversation above is reproduced, verbatim, from my journal.

Wilbur the pig left his mark, whether she remembers it or not. But has it blighted her life? I doubt it. She is a beautiful and fulfilled young woman, doing precisely what she ought to be doing. I am convinced that all the Wilbur the pigs of her life have helped prepare her to be the mature human being which she is; I have a vast amount to learn from the maturity of my first-born child.

There are many ways of thinking about how much we should, or should not, protect our children from the rough facts of life. It's said that the greatest single thing the Greeks contributed to civilization was giving us: "on the one hand" and "on the other hand." So what I am saying, no matter how categorically I state it, is simply "on the one hand," and a very fallible hand it is. The older I grow, the more grateful I am for the fact that there is far less overprotection of our children, at least in the book world, than there was a decade ago, even while I quite openly admit that Wilbur the pig, evil witches, ravenous foxes, *do* leave their marks on children.

But do we want unmarked children? Are they to go out into the adult world all bland and similar and unscarred? Is wrapping in cotton wool, literary or otherwise, the kind of guidance we owe them?

My mother lived a wild kind of life in her day. She may be a *grande dame* now, but in her youth she rode camels across the desert, watched ancient religious rituals from a Moslem harem, was chased by bandits down the Yangtze River. During one time of crisis, her best friend, who grew up as unscarred as it is possible to grow, came to offer help and sympathy, and instead burst into tears, crying, "I envy you! I envy you! You've had a terrible life, but you've *lived!*"

Once more: I don't mean that we should turn our children

out of the nest at the age of two to earn their own livings; no pre-school gin or *Lady Chatterley's Lover*; we do need a sense of timing; and where we seem to have been off in one direction a year ago, now we're overbalancing in the other direction. Alan showed me the outline for the Religious Knowledge course for the tenth grade at one of the more famous boys' schools in New England. The general title was: The Problem of God, from Aristotle to Sartre.

Sorry, whoever you are who went to great pains to make this outline, but I think this is sheer madness. Even a postgraduate student working for an advanced degree in theology could hardly cover the Problem of God from Aristotle to Sartre in a semester. This kind of thing is more than likely to dispose of God forever as far as a tenth grader is concerned.

I feel the same way about schools which proudly announce that they are giving inexperienced students in one year the *Canterbury Tales, Paradise Lost,* the plays of Shakespeare, *and* the Victorian novel *and* the Russian novel *and* contemporary French literature *and. . . .* The result is that the kids often don't read the books at the right time because they think they've already read them. We do owe our children intelligent guid-ance, mitigated by a sense of humor. There's a great deal of difference between guidance and censorship, though there's a thin line of demarcation and we can't always keep to it. We're going to fall off the knife's edge, one way or another. The best way to guide children without coercion is to be ourselves. Some-times we can fool adults about what we are; it's not so easy with children; they're going to see through us, no matter how elabo-rate our defenses. But this is one reason they're so exciting to work with; their vision is still clear.

Phillips Brooks said that "preaching is truth mediated by personality." Surely one can substitute teaching for preaching. It's what makes teaching and preaching and writing an activity of a human being instead of a machine.

One morning in Ohio someone brought up the separation of church and state, and the fact that hymns and prayers are now forbidden in public schools, and I agreed with those who felt that any kind of religious proselytizing in a public school is an impertinence—an independent school, obviously, is another question.

"But," I found myself saying, "you will find that you cannot help teaching children your own religion, whatever it is. If you are an atheist, that will be clear to them, even if you think you're teaching nothing but social studies. If a belief in God motivates your life, the children are going to know that, too, whether you ever mention God or not. If you are more interested in money than anything else, that's not going to escape them. You've got to accept the fact that you are basically not teaching a subject, you are teaching children. Subjects can probably be better taught by machines than by you. But if we teach our children only by machines, what will we get? Little machines. They need you, you as persons." And I quoted Emerson: "What you are speaks so loudly over your head that I cannot hear what you say."

So I know, with a sense of responsibility that hits me with a cold fist in the pit of my stomach, that what I *am* is going to make more difference to my own children and those I talk to and teach than anything I tell them.

Perhaps the fact that I do not remember the teacher who accused me of copying that poem tells something about her: I do not remember her name; I do not remember what she looked like, the color of her hair or eyes, her age, or the kind of clothes she wore. I remember exactly what Miss Clapp looked like, her hair style, makeup, little idiosyncrasies of dress and manner which were wonderfully dear to me. But that other teacher: nothing. When she decided that I was neither bright nor attractive nor worth her attention, she excluded me, and this is the most terrible thing one human being can do to another. She ended up annihilating herself.

To annihilate. That is murder.

We kill each other in small ways all the time.

At O.S.U. we discussed dividing grades into sections according to so-called ability. Every teacher there was against it. Every teacher there believed that a student in the lowest group is rendered incapable of achieving simply by being placed in that group. "So I'm in the dumb group. That's what they think of me. There's no use trying, because they know I can't do it."

Murder.

I didn't try to learn anything for the annihilating teacher for just these reasons.

I worry about this. I worry about it in myself. When I am angry or hurt, do I tend to try to exclude the person who has hurt me?

I said that a photograph could not be an icon. In one strange, austere way there are photographs of two people in my prayer book which are icons for me. I keep them there for that precise reason. They are people I would rather forget. They have brought into my life such bitterness and pain that my instinct is to wipe them out of my memory and my life.

And that is murder.

I had, through some miracle, already managed to understand this, when I came across these words of George MacDonald's:

It may be infinitely less evil to murder a man than to refuse to forgive him. The former may be a moment of passion: the latter is the heart's choice. It is spiritual murder, the worst, to hate, to brood over the feeling that excludes, that, in our microcosm, kills the image, the idea of the hated.

Thank you, Grandfather George.

He has come to my rescue many times, has said to me just what I needed to have said in a moment of doubt or confusion. When I was a little girl my grandfather used to send me books from London each Christmas. The first thing I did was smell them, open them, stick my nose in them, because English printer's ink smells quite different from American: smell, and then read. I loved the English Children's Annuals with their mixture of story, information, and comic strips; I loved Oscar Wilde's fairy tales; and I loved George MacDonald, beginning with *The Princess and the Goblin* and *The Princess and Curdie*. Like all great fantasists, he has taught me about life, life in eternity rather than chronology, life in that time in which we are real.

And he has finally made me understand what lack of forgiveness means. I cannot stay angry; this is not a virtue in me; I am physically incapable of going to bed out of sorts with anybody. But, although I have not stayed mad, have I excluded? put from my mind the person who has upset me? It is this which is the act of unforgiving.

I will remember this, I hope, each day when I come upon those two photographs of two very separate and different people. So, yes: those images have moved from image to icon. They have within them more than they are in themselves; in them I glimpse, for at least a fragment of a second, the forgiveness of God.

The Greeks, as usual, had a word for the forgiving kind of love which never excludes. They call it agapé. There are many definitions of agapé, but the best I know is in one of Edward

Nason West's books: agapé means "a profound concern for the welfare of another without any desire to control that other, to be thanked by that other, or to enjoy the process."

Not easy. But if we can follow it, it will mean that we will never exclude. Not the old, the ill, the dying. Not the people who have hurt us, who have done us wrong. Or the people to whom we have done wrong. Or our children.

I wrote out this definition of agapé on the blackboard at O.S.U. I have written it on other blackboards, quoted it in lectures. It teaches me not only about forgiveness but about how to hope to give guidance without manipulation.

.. 8 ..

A play like *The Skin of Our Teeth,* a book like *Charlotte's Web* or *Alice in Wonderland* are not defined at either end by an age limit. A book that is *only* for grownups, or *only* for six-year-olds, or adolescents, may serve a purpose, but it is a limited purpose, and is usually bounded by its place in time and culture. The most exciting books break out of this confinement and can be read at any period in time, in any country in the world, and by a reader of any age. One Crosswicks summer our sixteen-year-old alternated happily between *Anna Karenina* and C. S. Lewis's *Narnia* allegories. Our fourteen-year-old read H. G. Wells, Ray Bradbury, and Louisa May Alcott. Our eleven-year-old read farm journals, and Captain Mayne Reid's travel adventures, books which had belonged to his great-grandfather.

I think that was the summer I was writing *The Moon by Night,* a story that, as far as travel line goes, is based on the ten-week camping trip our own family took. I read the children the first draft, and they said, "No, Mother, you've stuck too close to your journals. It isn't real yet." They were right. I threw it all out, started again, and let it become considerably more real.

I think this has something to do with violence to words in the sense that Alan was talking about it. The first draft was nothing but an image, a mirror vision, with no reality of its own. Out of the image the writer tries to wrest reality. Perhaps the writer must, like Alice, go through the mirror into the country on the other side.

And we get back to: What is real?

What, Yetta, is a self?

.. 9 ..

We talk about identities and lose them; it's something like looking the Gorgon in the face and turning to stone. In American education today we too often either emphasize the sciences at the expense of the humanities or we have permissive schools where the child is allowed to express himself without restriction. It's too early to gather statistics (ugh) about how many great artists have come out of permissive schools, but I doubt if either of the educational extremes produces the right weather for art.

I learned about both art and identity in my structured, unliberal schools, probably a lot more than if I'd been allowed to indulge in unlimited self-expression. When I first went to an English boarding school, writing again provided my salvation. We were never alone. If we wanted solitude it was thought that we must have some perverse reason. We had fifteen-minute bath "hours" three times a week: we were supposed to bathe modestly in our underclothes; I love nothing better than the glorious sensuous feeling of water on my body and would bathe in the normal way, then rush into my underclothes and dip under water, always afraid of being caught and held up as an example of American depravity (If I did anything wrong it was an international incident); while we were bathing, the matron was apt to peer either over or under the partitions.

We were never allowed in our rooms alone, or in the class-rooms. The only way to solitude was through the world of note-book, a story, a play. So we learned to concentrate. I earned my right to be a bit different—a writer of tales—over the incident of the chewing gum. The mistresses assumed that all Americans chew gum. "All Americans"—absurd generality: I was *me*. And one of my particular oddities is that I was one of the one in ten who is born without the tooth on either side of the two front teeth. Usually when this happens the second teeth are simply allowed to grow together. If the dentist had let this happen with me, it would have given my face a narrow look, so he made a gold upper plate on which were fastened two small teeth; while the mouth is growing, a permanent bridge cannot be used. It was easy for me to take my tongue and loosen the gold bridge, which covered the entire roof of my mouth, and I often did so. One morning at assembly, when the roll was being taken, I was happily sucking my gold bridge, and the mistress taking the roll call saw me, assumed that I was chewing gum, and snapped at me, "Come here." Obediently I walked up in front of the entire expectant school. She held out her hand. "Spit." I spat. She looked with horror at the gold bridge with the two small teeth.

After that moment of glory I was allowed to be good at writ-ing and bad at hockey and net ball. I wrote subversively in the classroom during actual lessons, or during our so-called "free" time in the common room, with all kinds of commotion going on all about me, records, arguments, noisy games. As a result of this early discipline, I can concentrate in any amount of noise. I wrote my first novel while I was on tour with a play, in dressing rooms, waiting in railroad stations, anywhere I had a moment to pull out my notebook and pen.

I am grateful for having been taught concentration so early. I don't need to wait for the ideal situation in which to write. Or for inspiration. Inspiration does not always precede the act of writing; it often follows it. I go to my typewriter with reluctance; I check the ribbon; I check my black felt pens; I polish my collection of spectacles; finally I start to put words, almost any words, down on paper.

Usually, then, the words themselves will start to flow; they push me, rather than vice versa.

Carl Van Vechten wrote, "While dining recently in a public dining room with Christopher Isherwood, we were approached by an eager youth who proceeded to ask 'literary' questions, firing them at us with alarming earnestness. We answered them as well as we could, but when he hit upon that cliché, 'Why do you write with a pen or on the typewriter? Why don't you dictate?' I knew how to answer directly and truthfully. 'An author doesn't write with his mind, he writes with his hands.' Isherwood, immediately struck by the validity of this statement, was also amazed by it. 'Have you ever said or written that before?' he demanded. I assured him that the remark was both spontaneous and pristine."

And true. I copied it in my journal in January of 1952, and even with all the innovations of simpler tape machines, cassettes, dictaphones, it still holds.

It is out of this world that poetry comes, and music, and sculpture, the tangible world of hard work, manual labor, of practicing finger exercises every day. As a storyteller my job is to tell a good story; to learn to do this so that I can, indeed, write "with my hands," I must learn everything I can about structure and technique; I cannot neglect my practicing.

An artist of any kind is like a violin which has to be tuned regularly; it doesn't stay in tune by itself. Any musical instrument has to be played, or it dies, quite literally. In Washington, D.C., there's a magnificent collection of ancient instruments, but they'd be valueless wood and catgut if the finest musicians —the men of the Budapest String Quartet, for instance— weren't brought in to play them regularly.

Alan plays the violin about as well as I play the piano, and we have a lovely time making music together; we sound to ourselves as though we were, say, Isaac Stern and Artur Rubinstein. Our family and friends are tolerant—for a while, at any rate; though sometimes at the end of a party, when it's time for the last guests to go home, Hugh or Josephine will suggest that Alan and I play some Bartók.

Music is our relaxation, not our work. We turn to music when we "feel" like it. But I cannot write just when I feel like it, or I will have nothing to write with. Like the violin, I must be tuned and practiced on constantly. This can sometimes be hard on family and friends, but it's essential, and I'm blessed with people who put up with my absent-mindedness when I'm in the middle of a book, and my vocal enthusiasm for the subject matter of my enterprise, which I carry far beyond the dignity of wife and mother—or grownup.

One spring I was going on delightedly about something while I was cooking dinner, and Josephine startled me by saying, "Oh, Mother, you're such a child." I must have looked appalled, because she flung her arms around me and cried, "But we love you this way! We wouldn't want you to be just any old mother." So I was comforted. But opening oneself to this kind of remark, true though it be, is one of the many hazards of having writing as profession and vocation. I really don't see how it can be anything but both, because it's the last thing any sensible person would choose as a profession, with the possible exception of Hugh's. We've always thought of the precariousness of our livelihood as being rather hard on our children, but I looked at the whole thing with fresh eyes when Alan, the first winter we knew him, stood at my desk in the Cathedral library and remarked, "I think you and Hugh live more existentially than most people."

I felt we'd made it: we, like Sartre and Camus and Kierkegaard, were existential; we were really with it. It doesn't matter that I'm still not quite sure what living existentially means, though I have a suspicion that it's not far from living ontologically, because it's one of those words that's outside the realm of provable fact and touches on mystery. Nothing important is completely explicable. After twenty-five years there is much about my husband which is still mysterious to me, one reason why marriage remains exciting. Friendship goes on as my friends and I make new and often painful discoveries about each other. A great work of art never palls because there are always new insights to be found: has anyone ever learned at what the Mona Lisa is smiling? Or what El Greco's St. Andrew and St. Francis are talking about across a gap of eleven hundred years? I was in *The Cherry Orchard* for two seasons, one on Broadway, one on the road. Chekhov had something new to teach me every single performance.

.. 10 ..

A word written with the hands: it is tangible: I can be careless with these hand-hewn words but not as careless as I often am with my tongue. I should be more careful how I use the word "thing." I use it in two totally opposing ways. For a person or a group or a government to treat people as things is a mortal sin. That's one meaning.

The other is equally important. In a sense, to use "thing" in this second way is to take it away as thing, for essentially there is no such thing as a thing. Or, every single thing, every possible thing, is holy. I see proof of incarnation everywhere I turn. Here in Crosswicks I see it in the purple smoke of the mountains; the dark blue of fir trees against the green of maples and dying elms; the strong, sarxy stink of manure freshly spread on the pasture. In New York I find it in the sight of a spindly, naked, dead-looking tree in the barren island on Broadway near our apartment, the bare branches suddenly bursting forth with magnolia blossoms in the spring: what courage! I find it in snow (even deadly snow) falling past the lamps in Riverside Park when we walk the dogs at night.

And then, both in Crosswicks and in New York, there are my special things, my Lares and Penates, like the white Buddha.

The Piano:

When I am stuck in writing a book, when I am stuck in a problem in life, if I go to the piano and play Bach for an hour, the problem is usually either resolved or accepted. I find, as I grow older, that I turn less to the romantics and more to the baroque composers, though they've always been my favorites. In college I asked if I could learn something with more *feeling* in it, and my professor gave me some Chopin. What I had really been wanting, of course, was Bach.

And I did, years earlier, discover counterpoint for myself. We were visiting my grandmother in the South. What I remember most about her big old house was that there was a small conservatory, always green-smelling and warm, and that there were birds in it; and I remember her white, cluttered bedroom, off which was a screened sleeping porch entirely surrounded by trees covered with Spanish moss and filled with the singing of birds; and I remember the music room, with double doors leading to the living room. I spent a lot of time there, the doors closed, and one evening after dinner I was leafing through some old music and came across a rondeau by Rameau. I hadn't been taking piano lessons for more than a year or so, and I will never forget the shock of joy with wh... I heard my left hand repeating what my right hand had been doing, heard both hands together, one starting the melody, the second coming in with it: the feeling of discovery, of sheer bliss, is still vivid.

Here in Crosswicks we have my mother's piano. It is older than I am, has become difficult to tune, is not always predictable. Keys stick. Notes do not always sound when struck. When we moved back to New York for the winters it was clear that the piano would not stand another transition. In any case, we did not want to empty the house completely; it still had to be Crosswicks.

For a while we lived in a lovely but almost empty apartment. My mother came up from the South to visit, and one day she said, "You do miss a piano, don't you?" Yes, I did. Desperately. We kept our eyes and ears open for a second-hand piano, and eventually found one which Mother bought for me. It was not a great piano, but neither am I a great pianist. For a good many years it was perfectly adequate. Then it got to the point where the bass sounded dead and the treble sounded tinny, and tuning didn't help it at all.

One evening we were at Tallis's for dinner. The friend who had cashed Emily Brontë's check and I were with him out in the kitchen. Hugh was coming up after rehearsal; had he been there he probably would have shut me up, but I was beefing about the piano, and said, "If one of your ritzy friends is breaking up a big house and wants to dispose of a piano, I'm in the market."

The following Sunday after church we were again up in Tallis's apartment, and he staggered us by announcing, "Madeleine, I've decided to give you my piano."

Hugh's response was, "You can't! Where will you put your pictures?" For the top of the piano was covered with dozens of photographs—friends, godchildren, people from all over the world, famous and infamous, majah, minah . . .

The piano is a Steinway grand. It came to Tallis from Austin Strong, the playwright. It has been played by Paderewski and Rachmaninoff. It has also almost undoubtedly been played by my mother, though none of us knew this at the time. Austin Strong was a friend of my father's; they were of the same generation, and they saw each other weekly at the Players Club. My mother was a splendid pianist, and one of my earliest memories is hearing her run through an opera score while friends from the Met stood around the piano and sang.

The piano is now in our living room in New York. Tallis quite often remarks that things know where they belong. And The Piano is quite definitely an icon. I am convinced that the fact that Paderewski and Rachmaninoff have played it affects my own playing; the first night it was in our apartment I took my bath while Hugh walked the dogs, but instead of going to bed, I wrapped myself in a huge towel and, unable to resist, went to the piano. When Hugh came in he began to fumble with the dials on the radio-phonograph control, which are out in the hall by the front door. "What are you doing?" I asked him. He answered in surprise, "Are *you* playing? I thought it was WQXR." Such was the effect of The Piano.

A circle is considered the perfect form of art. In a novel or play, the resolution of the story is usually hinted at in the first sentence. One contemporary painter is so convinced that in the circle perfection is to be found that he paints only circles; circles within circles, without circles, imposed on, across, through circles. The Piano, in a sense, has come full circle: from my mother's fingers to mine, and through our dearest friend.

If it is a thing it is a holy thing: hallowed by love.

. . 11 . .

Simply the fact of The Piano has taught me something about love, love in the ancient sense of charity. Here is another word which needs to be redeemed. Charity has come to mean to many people a human response which is cold, uncaring, grudging, unwilling to share, duty-bound, untouchable. Whereas true charity is reflected in the words of a song popular among young people: "See me, feel me, touch me, heal me." Our kids are once again trying to find out what touching people means. They are aware that it doesn't mean the empty embrace on greeting by two acquaintances who don't know each other nearly well enough for something as fiery as touch. I'm not sure that the kids understand equally well that it also has nothing to do with the vast, meaningless orgies which are now commonplace on stage and screen; we're so used to seeing the nude body, female breasts, masculine torsos, faces distorted in what's purported to be orgasm, that we are even less aware of them than we are of the destructive smog which we breathe daily in our cities—but these scenes are part of the smog.

Hugh and I went the other night to one of these films, a wildly imaginative, beautifully photographed, two hours of obscenity; obscene's root meaning is *off-stage;* that which should not be seen on stage. Take the obscenity, in this meaning, out of that film, and it wouldn't have lasted five minutes. As we left the theatre, I said to Hugh, "If only there'd been some simple, healthy ——ing or ——ing on the screen, it would have been a clean relief." Later on, when I felt more reasonable, I said, "The extraordinary, awful thing about that movie was that in spite of all the sex shown, all the homosexual and nympho-maniac orgasms, nobody *touched* anybody else. Not once."

We have forgotten how to touch each other, and we try des-perately to do it in wrong, impossible ways which push us further and further apart. Sometimes when Hugh and I are in a large group I need to touch him; the only way this touch can be realized is if it is tiny and unobtrusive; if I put my arms around him in the middle of a cocktail party we wouldn't touch at all. But if I stand by him and let my finger brush momentarily against his, we meet; we are together. Too many of us have forgotten that this tiny gesture, this incredibly potent flame, can be as powerful an act of love as any other. We impoverish our lives when we limit our expressions of love. Alan said once, im-patiently, "Why are people so hung up on genitalia?"

I have a strong suspicion that all the emphasis on the superfi-cialities of sex, on allurement, on catching one's man, on wow-ing a girl, ends up destroying what they so shrilly advocate. We all know that a marriage based solely on the pursuit of pleasure doesn't often last long; we cannot spend all our lives in bed.

What concerns me most in the present prevalent freedom—no, not freedom, license, which is a very different thing—about the act of sex, is blunting the particular. If bedding becomes a series of one-night stands, it becomes a general thing-in-itself, instead of a very particular act between two particular, unique, irreproducible, irreplaceable persons. When it becomes a thing-in-itself, it is reduced to the de-personing realm of the general, which I presume is where Madison Avenue wants it; replace that powerful four-letter word, love, with the weaker three-letter word, sex, and people will buy more of our contemporary aphrodisiacs: faster and more lethal automobiles; more anti-perspirants (my mother once met a woman whose husband was one of the biggest deodorant manufacturers in the country; she let slip that he was also an ex-undertaker, and his product was made of embalming fluid), toilet water to replace the real aphrodisiac body odor of the clean and healthy male and female; buy, buy, buy, and you will be more attractive, more seductive, more like everybody else: more general.

The Greeks in their wisdom had four words for our one, *love*: there was charity, agapé; sexual love, eros; family love, storgé; friendship, philia.

But charity, agapé, really covers them all; if the other three don't also partake of charity, they go sour.

How do we loosen the noose? How do we recover charity? Please, my friends, do not turn off, do not slam doors when I call it Christian charity. Perhaps this means the opposite of what you think, the opposite of what we are.

In a brilliant article on a recent Fellini film, Gilbert Highet remarks that we are about to enter the post-Christian world. I am no good with chronology, but it seems to me that we have been in the post-Christian world since 1054 when the Eastern and Western worlds split, or maybe even earlier when Constantine made Christianity mandatory instead of dangerous and forbidden. Many people who have rejected the church today have done so because the establishment which calls itself Christian so often behaves in an unchristian manner; because, in the name of Christ, we have so often been intolerably cruel to other human beings. Too many priests and ministers have been seduced by the post-Christian world. Within it, however, lies the tiny, almost extinguished flame of the Christian world, kept alive by the often ignored remnant. If I do not feel despair at the state of the world today it is because I have an eager hope that the Christian world is going to be born again—not a reversion to the first years, but a breaking forth into something new and living and brilliant.

Half the congregation at the Cathedral on Sunday is under thirty; lots of them are long-haired and barefooted; lots of them aren't Episcopalian or any other so-called Christian denomination. But they are looking for the rebirth of Christianity. So are the kids in communes, though many of them aren't looking in the right places—but they are looking. Perhaps our age will not produce the great prophet, like Isaiah, that we seek; but I'm not at all sure that we haven't already produced unrecognized prophets of considerable stature. Prophets are seldom popular in their own day. Perhaps the Christian world I look towards will not be called Christian; the powers of darkness may have succeeded in trampling on the Name so that we will not be able to recognize it again for a great many years. I think the name does matter, and I keep listening for it.

There is a group of young ex-drug addicts in California called the Jesus Freaks. They have turned against drugs, and the transitory values of the world around them. I have met a group of Jesus Freaks in New York. They are, in an ancient, Pentecostal sense, trying to find truth, and what love really means. I'm not sure that they're looking in the right direction—though they may be. The important thing is that groups of Jesus Freaks should exist in the nineteen-seventies at all. There weren't any around in the sixties. Something extraordinary and new is emerging, and it gives me hope.

One spring one of my students showed me her notebook, in which she had written, "The only good artist is a dead one. All artists should be shot after they have finished producing. If they are allowed to live, they will start commenting on their works, and I have never heard an artist say anything intelligent about what he had done. . . . Beethoven had the right idea: he played one of his sonatas for someone, and when he had finished, the person said, 'That's very nice, but what does it mean?' And Beethoven sat down and played the whole thing over."

She wasn't being insulting; she was being accurate. I'm incapable of saying anything intelligent about anything I've written. When anybody asks "What are you writing about now?" if I try to reply, the book-in-the-works sounds so idiotic to me that I think, 'Why am I trying to write *that* puerile junk?' So now I give up; if I could talk about it, I wouldn't have to write it.

Dmitri Mitropoulos was asked if he could explain the extraordinary effect his conducting had on orchestra and audience alike, and he answered that he wouldn't even try to explain it, for fear that he might become like the centipede who was asked by a humble little bug which of his hundred legs moved first when he walked. The centipede, responding to the admiration with immense pride, began to analyze the question, and has not walked since.

Bug or centipede, we're apt to get tangled up in legs when we begin to analyze the creative process: what is it? why do people write—or paint—or sing?

If I grope for an answer, I glimpse it only in parable. There's a story Quinn told me which says a lot to me:

While he was at Yale Divinity School, he and all the young married students were given the opportunity of spending an informal evening with a well-known child psychologist. They were free to ask him anything they wanted to about children and family life, and one of the young mothers wanted to know why it is that everything in the household seems to fall apart around dinnertime.

The doctor answered, "You yourselves know the obvious reasons: the children are tired; it's the end of the day; they're hungry; they're ready for bed, so they respond by being whiny and fractious. You're tired, too—you've been struggling with diapers and formulas and housework, and you're apt to be edgy and short-tempered. Your husbands, coming home from their day's work, are also tired and not at all interested in hearing about your domestic problems, and they respond to the five o'clock tensions by being irritable and often not as understanding as they might be otherwise. These are the obvious reasons and you all know them. The real reason—" and here he stopped and said—"you will probably want to contradict me—the real reason is that we are all afraid of the dark."

There was indeed a clamor of contradiction, and the doctor responded by saying, "The very violence of your reaction proves the truth of my words."

Not long after Quinn had left Yale and become minister of the Congregational church here in the village, he held a meeting for mothers of nursery-school-age children, and several of the mothers brought up a problem that had been bothering them: what do you do or say to your children when they're afraid to go to bed in the dark?

There was a long and troubled silence. Finally one of the mothers who was a little braver than the others stuck out her neck: "You give him a night light."

I'm afraid of the dark—not afraid to go up the stairs in the physical darkness of night, but afraid of the shadows of another kind of dark, the darkness of nothingness, of hate, of evil.

So we rush around trying to light candles. Some are real: books are candles for me; so is music; so is friendship. Others blow up in our faces, like too much alcohol and too many sleeping pills or pep pills. Or hard drugs. Or sex where there isn't any love.

I think it was Toynbee who said that we are a sick society because we have refused to accept death and infinity. Our funeral practices open themselves up to satire, but they are only a symptom. There's an insurance commercial on the radio which says, "If something should happen to you," with the implication that without some unforeseen accident of course you'll never die. I am acutely uncomfortable when people talk about "passing away" because they're afraid to say "die." When I die I will die; I won't pass away, or pass on, or pass out. I will die.

Small children do not yet have a sense of chronology and therefore live in eternity; they are far more willing to accept death than we are. When his dearly loved grandfather died, our young son shut up like a clam. It seemed to his older sisters that he didn't care. We said, Wait. That night during his prayers he reached the point in his "God bless" prayer when it was time to name his grandfather, and stopped. He started over, came to the same point, and stopped again. Started once more, and finally said, "And God, please take care of Grandfather wherever you want him to be, another star or wherever you think, and make him be all right, and we love him. Amen."

I think I was even more relieved than the girls that he had not been indifferent, or shoving death away, but had been thinking, accepting.

Red, a seventeen-year-old boy who lived in our building in

New York, often dropped into our apartment shortly before dinner. He was an only child, and our normal noisiness appealed to him. And he liked to wander into Hugh's and my room, where I had my desk, and talk. One evening he came in as I was, as usual, banging away on the typewriter. "Madeleine, are you afraid of death?"

I turned around. "Of course, Red."

"Thank God. Nobody's ever admitted it to me before."

I've had people tell me they aren't afraid of death. I don't think I believe them any more than I believe writers who tell me they don't care what anybody thinks of their work. My agnostic faith does not, at its worst, include pie in the sky. If it runs along the same lines as does William James's, it cannot evade acceptance of responsibility, judgment, and change. Whatever death involves, it will be different, a venture into the unknown, and we are all afraid of the dark. At least I am—a fear made bearable by faith and joy.

The same spring that Red asked me that question, Hugh was on tour with a play, and Bion, with a high, undiagnosed fever, had to go to the hospital. Various loving (though misguided) friends, knowing that he missed the animals at home, brought him two goldfish and two turtles. He had been home from the hospital only a few days when both goldfish were found floating on top of the water. Being of a scientifically skeptical turn of mind, he refused to accept our verdict and insisted on waiting for the doctor's afternoon visit. The doctor's properly certified pronouncement of death was accepted, and we then had an elegant burial at sea, all of us walking the length of the hall singing a lugubrious hymn and then solemnly flushing the goldfish down the toilet. Amen.

The turtles grew and flourished. I tended them while the children were at camp. When we spent a few weeks here at

Crosswicks the change of water didn't agree with the turtles, so I took a bucket and went a mile to a spring-fed pond, and the turtles survived. But the following spring James, the younger of the two, began to suffer from soft-shell. Bion got advice from the neighboring pet shop and gave both James and Elroy, the elder turtle, baths in a special anti-soft-shell solution. In spite of this, one day when he came home from school we had to tell him that James was dead. Now, a turtle can be a very important thing to a small boy. He had kissed James and Elroy when he went off to camp (have you ever tried kissing a turtle?) and greeted them joyfully on his return. And even if, because of school and his roller-skate ice-hockey team, he sometimes forgot to change their water or to feed them, they mattered to him. James's death was a real blow. He went into his room and flung himself on his bed and sobbed. By dinnertime he had recovered and was quite philosophical and cheerful. "I think it did me good to cry. I got it off my head."

But when it came to disposing of the remains he was quite definite. James could not have a burial at sea like the goldfish, who had been members of the family for so short a time, and who were, after all, fish. James, he announced, had to be taken up to Crosswicks come summer, and be buried in the apple orchard "where he belongs."

"But," we protested, "we aren't going to the country for weeks. We can't just keep James till then. He'll smell."

Bion was calm but definite. "Then we'll have to preserve him. The animals in Jo's biology set are in preservative."

Well, I ended up freezing James. I wrapped him in aluminum foil, put him in an envelope, sealed it, marked it James, and put it in the refrigerator. Every time I defrosted, there was James, and usually at dinner someone would crack, "Turtle soup tonight, Mother?" But we did take James up to Crosswicks and bury him in the orchard, ringing a dinner bell to give the procedure proper dignity.

Our old collie, Oliver, died this past winter. It had always been understood that when Oliver died he would be buried in the Canon's Yard at the Cathedral, near his old friend, Tempête, Tallis's English setter. But Oliver died in midwinter when the ground had been frozen solid for weeks. There was no possible chance that a grave could be dug for him. I asked the veterinary who had given him his final shot what was the usual procedure, and he began going on about dog cemeteries and cremation urns. I was still standing in the office with the old dog lying on the table. I had stayed with him, my hand on him, while the shot took effect, and this had surprised the vet: "Most people don't want to see it. They're afraid." And then he started talking to me about the sickening sentimentality of dog ceme-teries. I said, "Oliver needed me while he was dying. He doesn't need me now. I'm not sentimental about his body. What is the simplest thing?" "The city will pick him up and cremate him and dispose of the ashes." "All right. Please have that done." It cost ten dollars, I think. It was all quite simple and, under the circumstances, right and proper.

But I found, later on when I got around to feeling, that I did mind, I minded badly, that Oliver wasn't buried in the Canon's Yard with Tempête.

I am neither logical nor theological about this. I don't have the word about it at all.

I am afraid of the dark.

And if I ask about this fear, do not offer me pie in the sky or talk to me in the narrow world of logical proof. Answer me, please, with the St. *Matthew Passion*; with *Twelfth Night*;

with *Guernica;* with simile and metaphor, image and icon. There isn't any other way to express or to understand anything which transcends material facts.

.. 13 ..

In these strange and difficult years since man has learned to split, though not to fathom the dark and dangerous heart of the atom, the attitude towards the language of myth has altered radically. It is the scientists themselves who have shaken our faith in their omnipotence, by their open admission that they have rediscovered how little they know, how few answers they really have.

Before they discovered nuclear fission and fusion, before they discovered the terrible fallibility this power revealed to them, many scientists were atheists; we don't need God if everything is explainable—in which case we would not need the language of the imagination and there would be no poets or storytellers. But on that day in 1945 in the desert in New Mexico when a group of men exploded the first atomic bomb, on that day when a light brighter than a thousand suns touched the sands of Alamogordo and those who had made it happen watched the mushroom cloud that has hovered over us ever since, this attitude changed. It is the scientists themselves who today are telling us that they cannot tell us everything—even as we walk on the surface of the moon, even as we probe into the strange and further field of genetics. The deepest scientific truths cannot be expressed directly. We hear this from men like Pollard, who has remained a distinguished scientist and has also become a priest. Fred Hoyle is a famous astrophysicist; but when he has an idea that goes beyond present knowledge (something very different

178

from wisdom) or that might upset some tired old pragmatic scientist, he turns to writing fantasy, where he can communicate ideas that are too big, too violent, too brilliant to be rendered directly.

The myths of man have always made it clear that it is impossible for us to look at the flame of reality directly and survive. Semele insisted on seeing her lover in his own form, as god, and was struck dead. In the Old Testament it is explicitly stated, many times, that man cannot look on the living God and live. How, then, do "myths" become part of experience?

In my church we observe, with considerable discipline, the season known as Lent. After its austerities, the brilliance of Easter will shine with greater joy. In the Jewish religion candles are lit, one each night for seven nights, for Hanukkah. The Hindus celebrate Dewali, the festival of lights, in which every house is ablaze with lights to rejoice in the victory of good over evil. In every culture there is a symbolic festival of light conquering darkness.

If we are not going to deny our children the darker side of life, we owe it to them to show them that there is also this wild brilliance, this light of the sun: although we cannot look at it directly, it is nevertheless by the light of the sun that we see. If we are to turn towards the sunlight, we must also turn away from the cult of the common man and return to the uncommon man, to the hero. We all need heroes, and here again we can learn from the child's acceptance of the fact that he needs someone beyond himself to look up to.

I feel about the cult of the common man somewhat as I do about restricted vocabulary and rapid reading. The common man lives within his capacity; he is probable as well as common; because of this he will choose the safe way. But mankind has progressed only when an uncommon man has done the improbable, and often the impossible, has had the courage to go into the darkness, and has been willing, out of the nettle, danger, to pluck the flower, safety.

Physiologically our backbones are not made for standing upright—one reason we human beings have so much back trouble. We have the backbones of four-footed animals, and had our ancestors limited themselves to their capacity, we would still be down on all fours, and therefore incapable of picking up a flower, a strange stone, a book, and holding it in front of our eyes.

But somewhere, sometime back in the far reaches of history, some uncommon man did the improbable, burst beyond the bounds of his capacity, and stood up on his hind legs so that his front paws were freed to hold something up to be looked at. And the road of evolution changed.

The uncommon man has done the impossible and there has been that much more light in the world because of it. Children respond to heroes by thinking creatively and sometimes in breaking beyond the bounds of the impossible in their turn, and so becoming heroes themselves.

But this is the Age, among other things, of the Anti-hero. This is the Age of Do-it-yourself; Do-it-yourself Oil Paintings: Just Follow the Numbers; Do-it-yourself Home Organ Lessons; Do-it-yourself Instant Culture.

But I can't do it myself. I need a hero. Sometimes I have chosen pretty shoddy ones, as I have chosen faulty mirrors in which to see myself. But a hero I must have. A hero shows me what fallible man, despite and even *with* his faults, can do: I cannot do it myself; and yet I can do anything: not as much of a paradox as it might seem.

In looking towards a hero, we are less restricted and curtailed in our own lives. A hero provides us with a point of reference.

Charlotte Napier, in *The Love Letters*, tries to explain this to João Ferreira: "Supposing you were sitting in a train standing still in a great railroad station. And supposing the train on the track next to yours began to move. It would seem to you that it was your train that was moving, and in the opposite direction. The only way you could tell about yourself, which way you were going, or even if you were going anywhere at all, would be to find a point of reference, something standing still, perhaps a person on the next platform; and in relation to this person you could judge your own direction and motion. The person standing still on the platform wouldn't be telling you where you were going or what was happening, but without him you wouldn't know. You don't need to yell out the train window and ask directions. All you need to do is see your point of reference."

Miss Clapp for me was a point of reference, not nearly as much because of what she taught me directly as because of what she was.

All teachers must face the fact that they are potential points of reference. The greatest challenge a teacher has to accept is the courage to be; if we *are*, we make mistakes; we say too much where we should have said nothing; we do not speak where a word might have made all the difference. If we are, we will make terrible errors. But we still have to have the courage to struggle on, trusting in our own points of reference to show us the way.

I once gave an assignment to a very assorted group of eleventh and twelfth graders to write a character study of someone they truly admired. They had been coming up with a strong crop of villains, and I pointed out that it's lots easier to write a villain than an admirable character, and I wanted them to try a positive, rather than a negative, character study. It didn't have to be anyone living; it could be someone from any time in history who was, to them, truly admirable; or it could be someone from fiction, a novel or a play or an epic poem; or it could be someone completely imaginary, their own ideal of what an admirable person ought to be. It was one of the least structured assignments I'd given them.

One of the boys, black and brilliant, had already admitted to me during a conference that his first reaction to almost any situation was resentment. It was obvious that his own feelings of hate and anger were disturbing to him—this was before militancy was as general and as accepted as it is today—and that he wanted to get rid of them. He was very open in discussing his problems but, even while he was asking for help, he was pessimistic about solutions. When he handed in this particular paper he had done part of a character study of someone who, I felt, turned out to be quite unadmirable. At the bottom he had written, "I'm terribly sorry about this paper. I really tried, but I can't do it. I can't think of anybody I admire."

The other kids made suggestions: John F. Kennedy; Abraham Lincoln; Martin Luther King; Marie Curie; Cesar Chavez. He listened politely but not one name drew a real spark from him.

No wonder he is unhappy and confused! To be sixteen years old and have nobody to admire means to have no point of reference. I know that he was then and undoubtedly is still running into situations where a reaction of resentment is almost inevitable. And what can one do to help? In terms of action, not very much. All I knew to do was to care about him, and to show him that I cared. When I walk through the streets of the Upper West Side of New York, my own little gestures of love in this angry world seem sadly inadequate. But they are all I have to give, and I am just falling prey to thinking that I can—or ought—to do it myself, if I underestimate them.

St. John said, "And the light shineth in the darkness; and the darkness comprehended it not." The light shines in the darkness and the darkness does not understand it, and cannot extinguish it (I need the double meaning here of the word *comprehend*). This is the great cry of affirmation that is heard over and over again in our imaginative literature, in all art. It is a light to lighten our darkness, to guide us, and we do not need to know, in the realm of provable fact, exactly where it is going to take us.

Alexander Schmemann, the Russian Orthodox theologian, says that Pope John XXIII's greatness lay in his not being afraid to open himself up to ideas that could not be contained in neat parcels, in not having to see the end of a road in order to have the courage to take the first steps.

We tend, today, to want to have a road map of exactly where we are going. We want to know whether or not we have succeeded in everything we do. It's all right to want to know—we wouldn't be human if we didn't—but we also have to understand that a lot of the time we aren't going to know.

The young people I talk with are, themselves, taking the first steps on a road leading into the unknown. They are at that most difficult of beginnings, the beginning of their adult selves. Their increasing consciousness of this may be responsible for the fact that some of them refuse the challenge to step boldly out into the dark. Being somewhat (*somewhat!* I can hear my husband say) of an extremist myself, I tend to have more sympathy with complete opting out than with the search for security and fringe benefits. I have more hope that someone who has shouted, "Stop the world, I want to get off!" can get back on and enjoy the ride, than someone who wants more cushions. My sympathy is automatically with the rebellious student rather than with the authorities. I was told that I was denied Phi Beta Kappa on behavior. Certainly I fought, with a small group of other rebels, for all kinds of academic reform. The year after I graduated there was an article in *The New York Times* listing all the reforms we had fought for and crediting them to the member of the administration who had tried hardest to block our way. This struck me as wildly comic, though during the battles themselves I had failed to find this person amusing.

But because I have a violent temper, because I know just how devastating the results of my own violence can be when it is uncontrolled, I knew, even back in my schooldays, that trying to fight for right by violence wasn't right—for me. Is there a time when one *has* to fight with violence? My mind and emotions do not agree here. I still think violence should be the last possible weapon, used only when everything else has been tried. And even then . . . I don't know. Could Hitler have been stopped except by out-and-out war? I don't think so. On the other hand, it was Gandhi who toppled the British Empire, not the militants . . .

I listen to the news and hear of war and rumor of war, of crime and wanton destruction and loss of humanity, and think of Ionesco's brilliant play, *Rhinoceros*. It starts out in a small French village on a Sunday morning; everything is normal and ordinary; the people in the village are very much like the people we know, like us. Then a rhinoceros strolls through the village square, and this first rhinoceros is like a presage of plague, because the people of the village start, one by one, turning into rhinos; they are willing to give up being their particular selves, to give up being human beings, to become beasts. And one of the characters says, "Oh, why couldn't all this happen in some other country so we could just read about it in the papers?"

But it's happening here. There are rhinos wandering about our land, and it is the younger generation which is most apt to see them. No, that's too easy, that's not fair; we must not make any kind of chronological segregation here, any more than in old people's homes. It's not a matter of chronology. I am afraid of people of any age who are willing to be involved in distant generalities but shy away from particularities; and I suspect that most writers, artists, share my feelings, because we deal in particulars.

In *Two Cheers for Democracy* E. M. Forster says, "I hate the idea of causes, and if I had to choose between betraying my country and betraying my friend, I hope I should have the guts to betray my country."

This is a statement no good Communist should accept; a Communist will—or should—betray any friend, parent, child, for the party. When we choose a generality, an idea, a cause, instead of a person, when this becomes the accepted, the required thing to do, then it doesn't matter if villages are destroyed by bombs; traffic deaths become statistics; starving babies can be forgotten when the television is turned off; and there will no longer be anybody who will read or write a poem or a story, who will look at or paint a picture, who will listen to or compose a symphony. No young man will walk whistling up the street. No young girl will sing about the love in her heart.

. . 2 . .

Children can teach us by their instinctive particularity. They learn through the particulars of their senses, and I learn from them. My children see to it, for instance, that I am kept *au courant* with their music, and I like it, not because it is sometimes noisy and meaningless, but because it is trying to express in today's medium the hope that there is, somewhere, somehow, structure and meaning in the world.

"Listen to the words, Mother," they tell me. "Maybe you won't go for the music, but you'll like the words."

They are words which on first hearing may make little sense, but they are words which are trying to break through the restrictions of our blunted vocabulary. "See me, feel me, touch me, heal me," the song says. And another: "If you let me make love to you, then why won't you let me touch you?" The need for love, for community, for being together, for being, for *isness*, sounds loud and clear in these songs. There is a passion for peace, a hatred of violence, a trying to break through to the place where two people can reach out and hold one another.

Dangerous, I suppose. No wonder people left the Congregational church when the kids played their own music, sang their own words.

Our youngest child is perhaps more determined than the others that I like the music. On the other hand, not long ago, when he and his best friend came out to the Tower to see me, he asked what I was playing on the phonograph. "Couperin." "Cool. Can we borrow it?"

When Bion was in first grade, Hugh and I went to New York for three days to celebrate our anniversary. When we returned, the first-grade teacher came into the store and told Hugh that while we were away our son had seemed perfectly happy; there was no noticeable difference in his behavior. However, the children in first grade did a lot of painting, and Bion, while we were away, painted only in black. The day we returned there was again no noticeable difference in his behavior, but his paintings were a violent joyfulness of color.

It certainly gave us pause.

Painting, writing, acting, are for him, as for his parents, a sign of order and meaning in the universe, and in today's strange world. Whether we like this world or not, whether we consider it progress or not, whether we think it one of the most exciting and challenging times in the history of mankind or not, it is here. This is a fact we cannot change by any form of escapism, nihilism, secularity, or do-it-yourself-ism.

My mother has seen the advent of gas light to replace oil lamps, of electric light to replace gas. She has seen the advent of the telephone, wireless, cables, television, all our means of instant communication. She has seen the development of bicycles, automobiles, prop planes, jet planes, rockets to the moon. And she has seen the explosion not only of technology but of population; there are more people alive now on this planet than have died in all the time since the world began.

Can we produce a single human being like Leonardo, who could reach out into every area of the world of his day? Our children have never known a world without machines: dishwashers, washing machines, dryers, electric beaters, blenders, furnaces, electric pumps, saws, computers—there are more machines than we can possibly count; beware, beware, lest they take us over.

We can't absorb it all. We know too much, too quickly, and one of the worst effects of this avalanche of technology is the loss of compassion.

Newsprint is too small for me now; I listen to the news on WQXR. I find that I always listen carefully to the weather: this affects *me*. If there is some kind of strike going on in New York —there usually is—which will inconvenience me, I get highly indignant. I am apt to pay less attention when the daily figures for deaths on battlefields are given; it is too far away; I cannot cope emotionally. Occasionally it hits me hard when I hear the announcer say that there were *only* fifty-four deaths this week:

only? what about the mothers, wives, sweethearts, children, of the fifty-four men who were killed? But it has to happen close at home before I can truly feel compassion.

We are lost unless we can recover compassion, without which we will never understand charity. We must find, once more, community, a sense of family, of belonging to each other. No wonder our kids are struggling to start communes. No wonder they will follow insane leaders who pull them into a morass of dope or murder. If they have no heroes, if we don't provide guidance, they are open to manipulation.

Marshall McLuhan speaks of the earth as being a global village, and it is, but we have lost the sense of family which is an essential part of a village. During our Crosswicks years we had the reality of this belonging, despite divisions between old and new residents; if tragedy struck anybody in the village, everybody knew it, and everybody suffered with those who suffered: old and new, Republican and Democrat, Catholic and Protestant. Because the store was at the crossroads, across from church and firehouse and filling station, Hugh and I always knew what was going on.

"They say there was a first-grade kid hit by a car. Who was it, Madeleine?"

I knew, because someone had come, white-faced, into the store, saying, "I was on my way up from Clovenford, and there was this little kid lying all bloody on the road; she belongs to those new people who just moved into the old Williamson house." The little girl was in the same room in school with one of our children; I knew what she looked like; she was not just any child, but one, particular, little girl. I felt in body and bone, heart and spirit, the pain her mother must be feeling. I continued with my work, trying to pray on that deep, underneath level. And the whole village responded, as it always does in emergency. The husband was out of town; there were offers by other husbands to get in touch with him; the nearest neighbors wanted to spend the night with the mother so she wouldn't be alone; food, quantities of food, as always, was brought in. This was a tragedy with a happy ending; there was loss of blood but no vital injury. The child was back in school in a few weeks. But we cared. It was close enough to all of us so that we were able to have compassion in a way that most of us cannot for the babies dying of starvation, or earthquake, or war, all over the globe.

Compassion is nothing one feels with the intellect alone. Compassion is particular; it is never general.

. . 3 . .

One hot afternoon the fire siren rang and Quinn went with the firemen to the top of a steep hill where a car was burning; the flames were completely out of control, and inside the inferno was an entire family, a mother, father, and four children.

At his seminary, Quinn had been taught that God, being perfect, is impassible and cannot suffer. That evening he stormed, "If God didn't care, then I don't want him."

I cried out, "Of course he cared! He was there in that burning car. If he wasn't, then he isn't God."

General compassion is useless. An aloof, general god is useless. Unless we, too, are in that burning car, we are useless.

It is still taught in some seminaries that it is a heresy to think that God can suffer with us. But what does the incarnation show us but the ultimate act of particularity? This is what compassion is all about.

It's no coincidence that just at this point in our insight into our mysteriousness as human beings struggling towards compassion, we are also moving into an awakened interest in the language of myth and fairy tale. The language of logical argument, of proofs, is the language of the limited self we know and can manipulate. But the language of parable and poetry, of storytelling, moves from the imprisoned language of the provable into the freed language of what I must, for lack of another word, continue to call faith. For me this involves trust not in "the gods" but in God. But if the word God has understandably become offensive to many, then the language of poetry and story involves faith in the unknown potential in the human being, faith in courage and honor and nobility, faith in love, our love of each other, and our dependence on each other. And it involves for me a constantly renewed awareness of the fact that if I am a human being who writes, and who sends my stories out into the world for people to read, then I must have the courage to make a commitment to the unknown and unknowable (in the sense of intellectual proof), the world of love and particularity which gives light to the darkness.

I'm a bit worried about the present fashionableness of myth, about all the books and articles and definitions, about the fact that myth has suddenly become meaningful and relevant ("Come, ranks of devils, assemble, I have a new battlefield for you: myth: Infiltrate!"). The current brouhaha about myth is blunting our awareness of it, as our vocabulary has been blunted. But that doesn't make it any less a vehicle of truth. Overexposure may make us see, even more than usual, through a glass, darkly; but the violent truth of myth is still there for us. I begin to understand why parables are sometimes used to *conceal* truth; it is another of those illuminating paradoxes.

My white china Buddha can conceal as well as reveal truth; but somewhere in the maze in which I wander, the dead ends of selfishness, silliness, sadness, I am guided, and I do not need to know precisely how. We are finite human beings, with finite minds; the intellect, no matter how brilliant, is limited; we must go beyond it in our search for truth.

An atheistic professor at one of the great universities—Harvard, I think—told his students, "You shall know the truth, and the truth shall make you free." He also told them that he couldn't remember the source of this particular quotation, but no matter, it was terribly important.

Yes. But it isn't just enough to know the truth ourselves: it is not a secret to be hoarded. How do we dare hope to share it without blundering too deeply into falsehood?

One day we were sitting around the kitchen table drinking tea, and my husband and our ten-year-old son got into a heated argument about baseball. Bion said, "But, Daddy, you just don't understand." Hugh replied in his reasonable way, "It's not that I don't understand. I just don't agree with you." To which our son returned, "If you don't agree with me you don't understand."

Most of us feel this way. If you don't agree with me you don't understand. But it takes a child to admit it. Today there is much loose talk about communication and about truth, and little understanding of what either one of them is. The language, which is ontological rather than intellectual, has little to do with the "linguistic sciences," which tend to smother language, rather than doing Alan's kind of violence to it. The linguistic sciences' emphasis on simplifying communication produces the odd result of so complicating it that we evade it entirely. Communication is never easy, as we discovered at Babel.

The primary needs can be filled without language. We can eat, sleep, make love, build a house, bear children, without language. But we cannot ask questions. We cannot ask, "Who am I? Who are you? Why?"

One of our best writers of teenage books, someone whose work I deeply admire, wrote an article saying that he is not going to write for teenagers any more because his sons have now grown up, and teenagers have changed so that he no longer understands them.

I am horrified. He is implying that he no longer has a language in which to communicate with teenagers, because teenagers have changed; but it is not change that makes language invalid, it is refusal to change. Teenagers, like the rest of us, are always changing. Every generation is different. Teenagers during the time when the Black Plague was decimating the world were unlike young people who lived in less violent centuries. To say that you won't write for teenagers any more because they have changed makes no more sense than to say that you won't write for adults any more, because today's world is so different from the pre-bomb world. It also implies that you write differently when you write for teenagers than when you write for adults.

If you are a responsible writer, you don't. The same rules that apply to *The Brothers Karamazov* (my archetypical adult novel) apply to *Peter Rabbit* (my archetypical picture book). The same rules that apply to Dante's *Divine Comedy* apply to *The Wind in the Willows*. Mankind is always in the human predicament, and this is what people write about. A good children's book is not easier to write than a good adults' book, and it poses to the writer the identical problem of trying to communicate his vision in a language that is not obsolete. This doesn't mean using current slang, but finding a language that will still be understood when this year's catch phrases have been replaced.

One of the most helpful tools a writer has is his journals. Whenever someone asks how to become an author, I suggest keeping a journal. A journal is not a diary, where you record the weather and the engagements of the day. A journal is a notebook in which one can, hopefully, be ontological.

A little more pragmatically, a journal, at least one that is not written for publication, and mine most certainly are not, is a place where you can unload, dump, let go. It is, among other practical things, a safety valve. If I am in the slough of despond, if I am in a rage, if I am, as so often, out of proportion and perspective, then, once I have dumped it all in the journal, I am able to move from subjectivity to at least an approach to objectivity, and my family has been spared one of Madeleine's excessive moods. A journal is also a place in which joy gets recorded, because joy is too bright a flame in me not to burn if it doesn't get expressed in words. And it's where I jot down ideas for stories, descriptions of a face seen on a subway, a sunset seen over the Hudson, or our Litchfield Hills. If I need, when writing a story, to recapture a mood, there it is, ready to live again for me. On the empirical level, if we have a family argument about when or where something happened, and the others don't agree with me, if I say, "But I know I'm right this time, I'll go get my journal," they usually give up. If I've remembered not only the event but the journal it's in, I'm almost always right—at least about that. In most other arguments I'm wrong.

Sometimes, on the children's birthdays, they enjoy having me go back to an old journal and read to them about their birth, and about their early years. The journals *are* full of family snapshots—not taken by me, however. My husband says that he never even properly sees a batch of snapshots before I've pasted them in my journal. And of course a journal is inviolate; I may read sections aloud from mine, but nobody, not even Hugh, is allowed to touch them.

A journal is useful in precisely the same way for a children's book as for an adult one. At O.S.U. I kept remarking hopefully each day that possibly, before I left, I might have some kind of definition of the difference between an adult novel and a true children's book. I never did—at least nothing that satisfied me any more than my instinctive reaction on the panel: that I'm not bright enough to know the difference.

"Why do you write for children?" My immediate response to this question is, "I don't." Of course I don't. I don't suppose most children's writers do. But the kids won't let me off this easily.

If you want to raise my blood pressure, suggest that writers turn to writing children's books because it's easier than writing for grownups; so they write children's books because they can't make it in the adult field.

If it's not good enough for adults, it's not good enough for children. If a book that is going to be marketed for children does not interest me, a grownup, then I am dishonoring the children for whom the book is intended, and I am dishonoring books. And words.

Sometimes I answer that if I have something I want to say that is too difficult for adults to swallow, then I will write it in a book for children. This is usually good for a slightly startled laugh, but it's perfectly true. Children still haven't closed themselves off with fear of the unknown, fear of revolution, or the scramble for security. They are still familiar with the inborn vocabulary of myth. It was adults who thought that children would be afraid of the Dark Thing in *Wrinkle,* not children, who understand the need to see thingness, non-ness, and to fight it.

When I am feeling unsure about my writing, it is not because I am worried about the difference between adult and juvenile fiction, but because I am worrying that I am neglecting other responsibilities, and so misusing my freedom; I've gone through periods of confusion and downright stupidity. It was our eldest child, with her remarkable ability to see and accept what *is,* who said to me a good many years ago, "Mother, you've been getting cross and edgy with us, and you haven't been doing much writing. We wish you'd get back to the typewriter."

So I write whichever book is clamoring to be written, for children or adults. But which or what is the difference is still a mystery to me.

Sometimes I play around with the words "childish" and "childlike," but the difference between them has been pointed out to us so often that it has become part of that obvious to which I am prone. But don't let that stop me.

I am part of every place I have been: the path to the brook; the New York streets and my "short cut" through the Metropolitan Museum. All the places I have ever walked, talked, slept, have changed and formed me.

I am part of all the people I have known. There was a black morning when the friend who cashed the Emily Brontë check and I, both walking through separate hells, acknowledged that we would not survive were it not for our friends who, simply by being our friends, harrowed hell for us.

I am still every age that I have been. Because I was once a child, I am always a child. Because I was once a searching adolescent, given to moods and ecstasies, these are still part of me, and always will be. Because I was once a rebellious student, there is and always will be in me the student crying out for reform.

This does not mean that I ought to be trapped or enclosed in any of these ages, the perpetual student, the delayed adolescent, the childish adult, but that they are in me to be drawn on; to forget is a form of suicide; my past is part of what makes the present Madeleine and must not be denied or rejected or forgotten.

Far too many people misunderstand what *putting away childish things* means, and think that forgetting what it is like to think and feel and touch and smell and taste and see and hear like a three-year-old or a thirteen-year-old or a twenty-three-year-old means being grownup. When I'm with these people I, like the kids, feel that if this is what it means to be a grownup, then I don't ever want to be one.

Instead of which, if I can retain a child's awareness and joy, and *be* fifty-one, then I will really learn what it means to be grownup. I still have a long way to go.

So with books. A childish book, like a childish person, is limited, unspontaneous, closed in, certainly doesn't appeal to a true grownup. But the childlike book, like the childlike person, breaks out of all boundaries. Here again joy is the key. A decade ago we took the children through Monticello, and I remember the feeling we all had of the *fun* Jefferson must have had with his experiments, his preposterous perpetual clock, for instance: what sheer, childlike delight it must have given him. I fancy that Lewis Carroll was truly happy when he was with children, and especially when he was writing for them. Joy sparks the pages of *Alice,* and how much more profound it is than most of his ponderous writing for grownups. Mozart, in pain, unhappy, wrote sheer childlike joy: *The Magic Flute* is a gloriously absurd fairy tale. His piano sonatas sound deceptively childlike; they are as difficult to play as any music ever written.

Lewis Carroll may have thought that he was writing a book for a specific little girl; he was also writing for himself; mostly for himself. The children's writer clarifies things for himself, not by wrapping them up in tight and tidy packages, but in opening himself up to them. One of the greatest delights of writing is in seeing words we never expected appear on the page. But first of all we have to go through the fear that accompanies all beginnings—no, not fear, but awe: I am awed at my temerity when I sit down at the piano to play a Mozart sonata; I am awed when I sit down at the typewriter to start a new book and so step out into that wild land where the forgotten language is the native tongue. Then, and then only, when I have got my feet wet in a distant brook, as real as the one at Crosswicks, am I free to communicate to others what I have seen.

There is a lovely Talmudic story that when the Children of Israel reached the Red Sea, and Moses struck his staff on the shore, the waters of the sea did not part to let them through. The Israelites stood there at the edge of the water and nothing happened until one of the men plunged in. Then the waters rolled back.

. . 5 . .

Juvenile or adult, *War and Peace* or *Treasure Island, Pride and Prejudice* or *Beauty and the Beast,* a great work of the imagination is one of the highest forms of communication of truth that mankind has reached. But a great piece of literature does not try to coerce you to believe it or to agree with it. A great piece of literature simply *is.*

It is a vehicle of truth, but it is not a blueprint, and we tend to confuse the two. A vivid example of this confusion was evident in a faculty workshop I attended. The school which was the host for the day runs from nursery through twelfth grade, and there was a good deal of searching by the teachers of the little ones as to what it is safe to tell them. We all agreed that one must never lie to them, but there was considerable disagreement as to just what constitutes this "safe" truth.

I found myself, as always, trying to remind everybody that truth is not just provable fact, and that the children themselves don't have the trouble in recognizing this that we do.

A specialist, a Ph.D. who teaches college students how to teach little children, was brought in to give us a morning of lecture and discussion. She told us a great deal about helping the child to be at home in the material and sensory world, to know what is sold in supermarkets, to know how raisins feel, or a daisy petal. Everything she told us was of the utmost importance, because she was deeply concerned with the tangible world in which the children have to live and function. But she never went beyond it, and the world of the imagination was never mentioned. When I asked her if children were to be denied the world of fantasy and myth and fairy tale, she had no answer. Of course they need fairy tales: she was willing to concede this at the same time that it was apparent that these stories had, for her, no place whatsover in the so-called *real* world for which she was trying to prepare teachers to prepare children.

This delightful professor (and she was delightful, though I have a suspicion she might not be amused at being called a Phid) is not an unusual children's specialist. I have met her—as it were—all across the country. There are thousands of her ilk, all full of degrees and facts and computed information, much of which is, indeed, vitally important. In schools all over the country there is a tremendous emphasis on preparing the child for the physical, material world, in giving him sensory experience, in taking him on field trips, in putting at his disposal all the latest discoveries in the world of fact, of preparing him for the world in which Euclidean geometry is true, where a table must have a solid top and be able to stand on its four feet, and where a square, even a human one, must be square.

But what is frightening is that far too many of these authorities on child guidance go on to tell us that anything beyond this pragmatic knowledge is not necessary, that anything else is *dishonest,* as a result of which many children today are growing up losing great areas of truth. The tragically comic thing is that these specialists are unwittingly contradicting themselves: they know that according to contemporary science Euclidean geometry is not "true"; a table is neither flat nor solid; and they emphasize the truth of Einstein's geometry and the new physics and biology as well as the new math.

Nevertheless, they are preparing the children to live in the functional Euclidean world exclusively, and keeping from them the vast open reaches of the imagination that led Einstein to soar out among the galaxies and bring back to us ever widening circles of truth. Just as we are taught that our universe is constantly expanding out into space at enormous speeds, so too our imagination must expand as we search for the knowledge that will in its turn expand into wisdom, and from wisdom into truth.

But this is violent, and therefore frightening.

Children are less easily frightened than we are. They have no problem in understanding how Alice could walk through the mirror into the country on the other side; some of them have done it themselves. And they all understand princesses, of course. Haven't they all been badly bruised by peas? And then there's the princess who spat forth toads and snakes whenever she opened her mouth to speak, and her sister whose lips issued pieces of pure gold. I still have many days when everything I say seems to turn into toads. The days of gold, alas, don't come nearly as often. Children understand this immediately; *why* is it a toad day? There isn't any logical, provable reason. The gold days are just as irrational; they are pure grace; a gift.

. . 6 . .

In one of his books, Edward Nason West tells of a time in his youth when he got so furious at another young man that he hit him. The other young man's response was a calm, "I see that words fail you."

What do we do when words fail us? They frequently fail me, and often when I'm using them in the vastest quantity, struggling to push through them to what I'm trying to express. Often they fail me entirely, as when young people ask me ultimate and unanswerable questions. It has been very helpful to remember that quite a few reputable scholars, including one Socrates, made a point, when asked such a question, of saying, "I don't know."

But children want to know, and perhaps it is our desire not to let them down that has led us into the mistake of teaching them only the answerables. This *is* a mistake, and we mustn't refuse to allow them to ask the unanswerables just because we can't provide tidy little answers. In our fear of the unprovable we mustn't forget that they can learn from *The Tempest* as well as social studies; that they can learn from Aesop as well as the new math; that *The Ugly Duckling* need not be discarded in favor of driver education. There is a violent kind of truth in the most primitive myths, a truth we need today, because probably the most important thing those first storytellers did for their listeners back in the dim past in their tales of gods and giants and fabulous beasts was to affirm that the gods are not irrational, that there is structure and meaning in the universe, that God is responsible to his creation.

Truth happens in these myths. That is why they have lasted. If they weren't expressions of truth they would long have been forgotten. One of the great historical pieces of evidence is the Bible, both the Old and New Testaments. Many books which were once in the Bible have dropped out of sight through the centuries. Those that have stayed with us are those that contain truth that speaks to us in our daily living, right where we are now.

In the beginning God created the heaven and the earth. . . . The extraordinary, the marvelous thing about Genesis is not how unscientific it is but how amazingly accurate it is. How could the ancient Israelites have known the exact order of a theory of evolution that wasn't to be formulated by scientists for thousands of years? Here is a truth that cuts across barriers of time and space.

So myth, fantasy, fairy tale contain an iconic truth, and in turning to their language we are not going backwards but forwards to that language which is not obsolete. We must not take from our children—or ourselves—the truth that is in the world of the imagination.

I look at the babies; we make daisy chains and play ring-around-a-rosy and put two candles on a birthday cake, and I wonder: what can we give a child that will stay with him when there is nothing left?

All we have, I think, is the truth, the truth that will set him free, not a limited, provable truth, but the open, growing, evolving truth that is not afraid.

. . 7 . .

During a panel discussion on drugs, homosexuality, pornography—"problems" in children's books—I suggested to the young teenagers on the panel that if they wanted facts about these subjects, they turn to non-fiction, to scientific articles. One of them asked, "But can't we find truth in fiction, too?"

"Who said anything about truth? I told you to check *facts* in non-fiction articles. If you are looking for truth, the place to look for it is exactly in stories, in paintings, in music."

We may find the facts about intercourse in an article; but we learn about love in that very contemporary play, *Romeo and Juliet*. We learn about insemination and childbirth in film strips and lectures; but we learn about creation in

> Tiger! Tiger! burning bright
> In the forests of the night,
> What immortal hand or eye
> Dare frame thy fearful symmetry?

It is an extraordinary and beautiful thing that God, in creation, uses precisely the same tools and rules as the artist; he works with the beauty of matter; the reality of things; the discoveries of the senses, all five of them; so that we, in turn, may hear the grass growing; see a face springing to life in love and laughter; feel another human hand or the velvet of a puppy's ear; taste food prepared and offered in love; smell—oh, so many

206

things: food, sewers, each other, flowers, books, new-mown grass, dirt . . .

Here, in the offerings of creation, the oblations of story and song, are our glimpses of truth.

. . 8 . .

One summer Hugh and I went, more or less by accident, to a burlesque show. We'd gone down to the Village to see an off-Broadway play in which a friend was appearing, found that he was out that night because he'd strained his back. We thought we'd rather wait to see the show when he returned to it, and directly across the street was a marquee proclaiming Ann Corio in *This Is Burlesque.*

"How about it?"

"Fine."

It was great fun. A series of pretty young girls came out on stage and danced while removing their clothing. I was filled with envy not so much for their lovely bodies as for the way they could twirl the tassels on their breasts: clockwise, counter-clockwise (widdershins!): it was superb.

Towards the end of the performance one stripper came out who was a little older than the others, possibly a little beyond her prime. But she had a diaphanous scarf in her hands, and she twirled and swirled this about her as she removed her clothes, and Hugh remarked, "She's beautiful." It was only she, of all the strippers, who gave the audience a feeling of mystery.

If we accept the mysterious as the "fairest thing in life," we must also accept the fact that there are rules to it. A rule is not necessarily rigid and unbending; it can even have a question mark at the end of it. I wish that we worried more about asking the right questions instead of being so hung up on finding answers. I don't *need* to know the difference between a children's book and an adult one; it's the questions that have come from thinking about it that are important. I wish we'd stop finding answers for everything. One of the reasons my generation has mucked up the world to such an extent is our loss of the sense of the mysterious.

One night after dinner a group of us were talking about the supernatural, and one of our dinner guests said that when the electric light was invented, people began to lose the dimension of the supernatural. In the days before we could touch a switch and flood every section of the room with light, there were always shadows in the corner, shadows which moved with candle-light, with firelight; and these shadows were an outward and visible sign that things are not always what they seem; there are things which are not visible to the mortal human being; there are things beyond our ken.

One of my favorite theologians is Albert Einstein. He writes, "The fairest thing we can experience is the mysterious. It is the fundamental emotion which stands at the cradle of true art and true science. He who knows it not, who can no longer wonder, can no longer feel amazement, is as good as dead, a snuffed-out candle."

Our younger daughter is engaged to a theoretical chemist who delights me in many ways, not the least of which is that he looks like Einstein, and, it seems to me, thinks like Einstein, too. He's finishing a post-Ph.D. grant at the University of Pennsylvania and showed me his most recent publication: "Look, Madeleine, nothing but equations! I'm getting rid of words entirely." When the world around him gets too much in his Einsteinian hair he murmurs, "All I want is to be left alone with my numbers."

He will learn, I am confident, that his numbers themselves will not allow him to stay alone with them, that they will shove him around, as words shove me (he may think he's getting rid of words, but his formulas are full of Greek letters). He is also learning the strange rules of the mysterious. Einstein writes, "What is the meaning of human life, or, for that matter, of the life of any creature? To know the answer to this question means to be religious. You ask: Does it make any sense, then, to pose this question? I answer: The man who regards his own life and that of his fellow creatures as meaningless is not merely unhappy, but hardly fit for life." He also says, "The true value of a human being is determined primarily by the measure and the sense in which he has attained liberation from self."

Science, literature, art, theology: it is all the same ridiculous, glorious, mysterious language.

It was while I was steeping myself in Einstein, Planck, and various other physicists and cosmologists during the writing of *Wrinkle* that I came across and was fascinated by the first law of thermodynamics, which is one of the rules of the mysterious. It tells us that energy and heat are mutually convertible, but if you get energy you lose heat, and if you get heat you lose energy. Or, to put it in non-scientific layman's language, you don't get something for nothing.

A science-fiction story tells of a machine that was invented that could produce everything needed for man's comfort on earth: food and furniture; refrigerators and radios; clothes and cars. There were a few wise men who warned people that one cannot continually take without putting back, or the supply will be depleted, but they were laughed at. After several centuries of the machine giving freedom from all material want, schools were teaching that the old myth that the earth was once larger than the moon was rank superstition. And at the end of the story there is one toothless old man clinging to a tiny and depleted fragment of earth.

How does the first law of thermodynamics apply to the making of books? Most of us realize that if we buy our groceries or gasoline from a place that gives trading stamps, we are paying for the trading stamps in higher prices. It may be fun, but it's not something for nothing. I trust that most of us are not like the woman who left her neighborhood market, paid thirty cents to ride a bus, went to another market, bought five pounds of sugar for which she paid one cent less than she would have in the first market, paid thirty cents to ride home, and was triumphantly convinced that she had saved money.

I'm not referring to the rising cost of books—that's another story—but to books which are afraid of the mysterious, leave nothing to our imagination, and try to break the first law of thermodynamics.

There are the four-letter-word books which have ruined our four-letter words. I was horrified recently to see the word "shit" irresponsibly used in a book for the ten to twelves, not because these children have never heard the word, but because these words, sex scenes, normal and perverse, have become big business and children's writers are joining adult (?) writers in cashing in on it. Something for nothing: there is no word, no action, which is of itself out of place if it springs from artistic necessity, if it is paid for by the fact that it is essential to the life of a story.

I am bored with the sex books which are demolishing sex—or trying to, because the intent is ultimately murder. Orville Prescott mentioned in a review, with a deep, figurative sigh, the sex scene that seems to have become *de rigueur* in the modern novel. This is a peculiar kind of perversion, this voyeurism. I'm totally against any kind of legal censorship, but I'm fed up with play-by-play descriptions of the act of intercourse. If we've made love, we don't need to be told about it; if we haven't, a description of its physiological progress isn't going to tell us anything. When the writer leaves something to the readers' imagination he is like the beautiful burlesque stripper who, with her diaphanous veil, added a sense of mystery to the human body.

The sexiest books I know, are those like *Anna Karenina* and *Phaedre;* or, if we want realism, what about that arch-realist, Flaubert? *Madame Bovary,* for instance: for sheer power in giving us the sense of uncontrollable physical passion no one can beat the scene in which Emma and her lover, Léon, get into a carriage, "a carriage with drawn shades," that is seen driving on and on through the streets, "sealed tighter than a tomb and tossing like a ship." The picture of this carriage with the drawn shades is far more sexually potent than any diagram of what was going on within it. In this climate of mystery, passion can flourish far more strongly than in the clinical glare of the laboratory.

Hemingway is not known for his reticence, and yet one of his most poignant love scenes is in *For Whom the Bell Tolls,* where Robert and Maria are together in the sleeping bag, and all Hemingway says is, "The earth shook beneath them."

Now some readers, both adolescent and supposedly mature, *are* looking for pornography. They come into bookstores and libraries hunting for substitute life, for vicarious sex. When they ask for books that pander to their desire for four-letter words, for descriptions of intercourse, for something for nothing, they're not unlike addicts looking for substitute pleasure.

Censorship is not the answer. I have intense respect for all the librarians and teachers who guide but do not manipulate. I know of at least one librarian who starts her readers on what they ask for, on what they think they want; then, when she gets to know them, when she has made friends, she offers something with a little more substance, and then, when that is accepted and swallowed, something with even a little more. And without exception, she says, when the real thing is accepted, the desire for the cheap substitute goes. Something for something is far more satisfying than something for nothing. "Take what you want, said God," runs an old Spanish saying. "Take it, and pay for it."

The taboos about death and sin which delayed some of my books' being published in the children's field have now been broken; it would seem that everything goes. But this is not quite true. When we break one taboo, we replace it with another. Alan remarked to me that just as we suffered from the sexual repression of Victorianism, so we are beginning to suffer from the spiritual repression of this century. Even in the church, the transcendent, the mysterious, the irrational in God is taboo; God is the Great Sociologist.

But: warning: there is, in art, no subject which is in itself taboo, either for children or adults. The way in which the subject is handled is what matters. The same subject can be obscene and repellent, or alive and loving, depending on the artist. And the reader. I had a troubled letter from a librarian in California who had received a number of phone calls from the parents of the high-school children who were passing *A Wrinkle in Time* around because of the sex passages. She gave me page numbers, and I rushed to the bookcase, eager to read my sex scenes. They were the descriptions of tessering. I wrote back that if one wants to, one can find sex symbols in anything, and I thought those in *A Wrinkle in Time* were probably healthier than those in some of the other books I knew high-school students were reading that year, and suggested that she relax about it.

I read lots of adult novels when I was a child; the parts about sex were mostly outside my vocabulary and definitely outside my experience; I didn't understand them and slid over them. Unless a grownup, looking horrified, tells us that we shouldn't read a book because it is "dirty," we, as children, won't even see the dirt because it is outside our field of vision; we have not yet been corrupted by repressive taboos. And children are a great deal less naïve and fragile than many adults give them credit for being.

Whatever the contemporary taboos may be, all great books are imbued with Einstein's quality of the mysterious, and keep its rules. Is this, then, going to enable us to tell, out of the large quantity of books published each year, which ones are going to join the ranks of the great and which will be forgotten? I doubt it. And I don't think this matters.

A truly great work of art breaks beyond the bounds of the period and culture in which it is created, so final judgment on a current book has to be deferred until it can be seen outside this present moment.

How, then, do publishers judge? A publisher has to use his sense of smell, and he has to be a hardheaded businessman, or he won't be a publisher for long. Not many make the mistake of the men in the television industry who wait with bated breath for the Nielsen reports, for Trendex, to tell them what the viewer wants, and then proceed to give the viewer more of what the calculating machine has ordained that the viewer wants. I don't think most people in the book business fall into the error of thinking that the machines, the public-opinion polls, the bestseller lists, know what the public wants. Then who does?

I do. You, my dears, do. Because we *are* the public. We do have to have faith in our own convictions. We are not machines, but living human beings who sign our own checks with our own names; and I have a lot more faith in us than I do in

Trendex. It is human beings who have the wisdom to spot a book that perhaps a publisher is *not* pushing, that gets ignored by reviewers, but that will still be selling long after the immediate success: examples: *Lord of the Flies. The Lord of the Rings. Narcissus and Goldmund.* Students, once they discovered these books, went wild over them, students who still had not lost sight of the particular in the forest of generalities.

Josephine's godfather is now an important man in the world of the English theatre. When he first started work in a London producer's office, hadn't been there very long, and didn't know many people, he was invited to a large and fashionable supper party. He was having a lovely time, because Toby always has a lovely time; he has complete and passionate interest in people. And he doesn't have to wait for anybody to tell him who's important at a party, whom he "ought" to be speaking to. In the midst of his pleasure he noticed a slender man sitting off by himself with nobody paying much attention to him. So Toby immediately went over to pay him some attention, to make sure that he wasn't unhappy. They got along famously, and after a while the quiet man identified himself as General Sir Frederick Browning, Comptroller and Treasurer for Their Royal Highnesses Princess Elizabeth and Prince Philip. He was also the husband of Daphne du Maurier, and one of the most "important" people at the party. He asked Toby if he'd like to go to Buckingham Palace the next day to see the Royal Art Collection and to have a guided tour of the whole palace. A few minutes later Gertrude Lawrence came up and said, "Toby, do you appreciate what an honor this is? I've known Boy for years, and he's never invited *me* to see the king's pictures." Of course Toby asked if he might bring Gertie too, but that's another story.

Toby isn't afraid to stick his neck out; he doesn't try to play it safe. He doesn't depend on Trendex rather than his own opinion. Because he is, thank God, human, he sometimes makes mistakes; but he wouldn't be where he is now if his opinion hadn't far more often been right than wrong. Or if he hadn't been willing to take risks for what he believes in.

One decade in the nineteenth century produced Hawthorne's *The Scarlet Letter* and *The House of Seven Gables,* Emerson's *English Traits* and *Representative Men,* Melville's *Moby Dick,* Thoreau's *Walden,* and Whitman's *Leaves of Grass,* and— reminds *The New York Times,* my source for this information —"none of these achieved more than a modest sale." In 1853 Thoreau was informed by his publishers that *A Week on the Concord and Merrimack Rivers* had sold 219 copies since its publication four years before, so they sent him the remainder. He wrote, "I now have a library of nearly nine hundred volumes, over seven hundred of which I wrote myself." That same year, seventy thousand copies were sold of a book called *Fern Leaves from Fannie's Portfolio.*

We never know when a book is going to be like the quiet man Toby found in a corner of the fashionable supper party, when it is going to turn out to be a Sir Frederick Browning. It's far more exciting to be enthusiastic about the real book that deals with life in all its particularity than to allow ourselves to be dazzled by the cheap substitute that tickles the palate for the moment but leaves us with a hangover. And all we have to rely on to tell the difference is ourselves, not a computer.

I'm all for realism in the book business, but I'm afraid of cynicism, and the two are often too close for comfort. Books must be sold, or there will be no more publishers, or booksellers, or librarians—or writers, majah, minah, or mediocah. We remember the reputable publisher who published a recent flaming best seller knowing that it stank—but that it would sell. We all know writers who write solely to make money, and this is a perfectly legitimate business. It is quite proper to render unto Caesar the things which are Caesar's. But there is something in us that knows that this is not enough, which reaches out for something more, which longs for Einstein's realm.

. . 9 . .

In Smith I majored in English literature, and one of the required courses was Chaucer. I loved him. It fills me with joy to know that Chaucer, with his explosive, bawdy, colorful imagination, changed the course of the English language. If it had not been for Chaucer breaking with tradition and writing in the language of the common people, instead of the more elegant Latin or French, we might be speaking a kind of bastard Norman today.

I wonder: if Chaucer hadn't come along, what would have happened to Shakespeare when he picked up his pen two hundred or so years later? There's an idea for a story, one day . . .

In the final exam in the Chaucer course we were asked why he used certain verbal devices, certain adjectives, why he had certain characters behave in certain ways. And I wrote, "I don't think Chaucer had any idea why he did any of these things. That isn't the way people write."

I believe this as strongly now as I did then. Most of what is best in writing isn't done deliberately.

Am I implying that an author should sit around like a pseudomystic in his pad, drinking endless cups of espresso and smoking pot and waiting for enlightenment?

Hardly. That isn't how things happen, either.

Hugh and I heard Rudolf Serkin play Beethoven's *Appas-*

sionata sonata in Symphony Hall in Boston many years ago. It was one of those great, unpredictable moments. When the last notes had been lost in the silence, the crowd not only applauded, cheered, stamped, we stood on our chairs: this doesn't happen often in Boston.

But if Serkin did not practice eight hours a day, every day, the moment of inspiration, when it came, would have been lost; nothing would have happened; there would have been no instrument through which the revelation could be revealed.

I try to remember this when I dump an entire draft of a novel into the wastepaper basket. It *isn't* wasted paper. It's my five-finger exercises. It's necessary practicing before the performance.

.. 10 ..

I am often asked how I came to write *A Wrinkle in Time*. Even with all the hindsight of which I am capable I can't quite explain it. It was during a time of transition. We had sold the store, were leaving the safe, small world of the village, and going back to the city and the theatre. While we were on our ten-week camping trip from the Atlantic to the Pacific and back again, we drove through a world of deserts and buttes and leafless mountains, wholly new and alien to me. And suddenly into my mind came the names, *Mrs Whatsit. Mrs Who. Mrs Which.* I turned around to the children and said, "Hey, kids, listen to these three great names that just popped into my mind; I'll have to write a book about them."

But why did those names come to me just then, and from where? I haven't the faintest idea. I suppose that my writing mind, which is always at work no matter what is happening on the surface level, took over from there. I had brought along some Eddington, some Einstein, a few other books on cosmology—I was on a cosmological jag at that time, partly, I suppose, because it satisfied my longing for God better than books of theology; and the influence of these books on *Wrinkle* is obvious. I was also quite consciously writing my own affirmation of a universe which is created by a power of love.

When the book was rejected by publisher after publisher, I cried out in my journal. I wrote, after an early rejection, "X turned down *Wrinkle,* turned it down with one hand while saying that he loved it, but didn't quite dare do it, as it isn't really classifiable. I know it isn't really classifiable, and am wondering if I'll have to go through the usual hell with this that I seem to go through with everything I write. But this book I'm sure of. If I've ever written a book that says what I feel about God and the universe, this is it. This is my psalm of praise . . ."

And again, "And yesterday morning before we left, there was a letter from Hugh saying that X has turned down *Wrinkle.* Perhaps I'm slowly becoming inured. I went through a few hours of the usual primitive despairing rage, but I could show none of it as I was with the children driving down to the city. Am I really getting so that I can stand it better? Perhaps the fury and bitterness builds up. But all there is today is a heaviness that makes all household chores wearily difficult. All work seems a little harder . . . In a book I'm reading about Fitzgerald, there is a sentence about 'second-rate writers who pass themselves off as geniuses.' But how does anybody know? A writer is far too tied up in his work, if he is really a writer, to know whether it is second-rate or a work of genius. And how many writers who have been considered second-rate, and yet have persisted in believing in themselves, have been discovered and hailed as geniuses after their deaths; or writers who have been highly acclaimed during their lives have been forgotten forever shortly after? or writers who are true geniuses have never been discovered at all? Does it really matter if we are geniuses or second-rate? If we are majah, minah, or mediocah? As for *Wrinkle,* for once I have the arrogance to know in my heart that this is something good. But if it is constantly turned down will I be able to keep the faith that I still have in it? Will I begin to doubt?"

I'm ashamed of all the wailing, but I did it. "Why do I love this Tower so when I have done so much bitter weeping in it? X has turned down *Wrinkle,* too, and this has really thrown me. I cared terribly about having them take it, and they turned it down so quickly, two days, that I know it hasn't had a fair reading. Someone lower down who just sent a form-type of rejection. This is one of the times when I think I'm yelling with complete and utter reason."

Does it sound as though I use my journals for nothing but weeping and wailing and gnashing of teeth? I don't. Much of this book is right out of the pages of my journals, those everything-books, and much from the scribbling of this summer just passing. And I don't mean to dwell on failure and bitterness and rejection. If I bring it up again here it is for two reasons: it may give a little courage to someone else who is going through a similar stretch. And I know now that the bleakness of that period of my life, bleak in many areas, was an essential part of my growing up, both as a woman and as a writer. And in the midst of the bleakness I could write—a few days after one of the *Wrinkle* rejections—"I've been writing hard on the new book, and am tired and happy." And, "Here I am in what would certainly be considered my middle years, and yet I feel as young and eager and open to development as I did when I was twenty-one."

It was a long time after these fairly close-together entries that *Wrinkle* went to Farrar, Straus and Giroux. I worked on what was eventually to become *The Love Letters*. I recorded a happy evening of singing rounds at the table. I worried about not being a good enough wife. Or mother. I was joyful. In misery. In other words, I suppose I behaved normally for a writer.

This was 1960. In 1963 when I was in Chicago to receive the Newbery Medal for *A Wrinkle in Time*, a woman who was a fine editor for me with *And Both Were Young*, but who had rejected both the *Austins* and *Wrinkle*, said to me, "I know I should have published these books. But I wonder: if I had accepted *A Wrinkle in Time*, would it have been the right moment for it? If it had been published then, maybe you wouldn't be here now."

She is a very wise woman.

The ancient Israelites, crossing the desert, missing the very imprisonment of the days in Egypt, taking too long to get to the Promised Land, wailed, "We remember the fish, which we did eat in Egypt freely; the cucumbers, and the melons, and the leeks, and the onions, and the garlick." They complained about the manna which had been sent them, and were angry and demanding. "Lust came upon them in the wilderness; and they importuned God. And he gave them their desire, and sent leanness withal into their soul," wrote the Psalmist.

Thank you, God, for not giving in to my importunate demands.

. . 11 . .

To balance the precarious triangle of wife-mother-writer: it was, is, a problem. And what did I mean by trying to "be good"?

To knock down selfishness, self-will, I suppose. And this is not a do-it-yourself job. We can no more "try" to be virtuous than we can try to be humble, or to act with integrity.

Virtue, that odd, old-fashioned word: we have all known so-called virtuous women, professional do-gooders, busybodies; they have no lives of their own, so they try to interfere with others.

How we have blunted this word which comes from the French: Cooper's *Thesaurus Linguae Romanae et Britannicae* says: "Vertue, strength, puissance, prowesse, valiantnesse, manlinesse, manhoode, power."

A description, surely, of the man every young girl seeks, the man strong enough to be gentle, powerful enough to be tender.

I am grateful to the virtuous men I have encountered in this world: my father who, in the trenches, would not send his men anywhere he would not go himself; he was known as "Bonnie Prince Charlie."

My husband, who has had the puissance and valiantnesse to put up with me for a quarter of a century.

The friends of my right hand.

.. 12 ..

They guide me with their virtue, particularly when I bumble into "I can do it myself." One day the children came home from school, bringing with them a discussion about precisely this: in an emergency one must not depend on law or on structure but on judging the situation as it arises, and then making the "loving" decision. We must meet each particular situation separately, with no general preconceptions. This is very well in theory, and it is paradoxical of me to have reservations, but I do.

What sends up those little red flags of warning is the assumption that in a crisis we will possess the calm reason with which to make the loving decision. It presupposes that man is perfectible of his own effort—just try a little harder, chaps, and it will be all right.

Collectively and separately my generation has tried pretty hard, and it isn't all right.

In a moment of crisis we don't act out of reasoned judgment but on our conditioned reflexes. We may be able to send men to the moon, but we'd better remember we're still closely related to Pavlov's dog. Think about driving a car: only the beginning driver *thinks* as he performs each action; the seasoned driver's body works kinesthetically; steering wheel, brake, accelerator— if you have to think about using each one of these you won't dare drive on a major highway. A driver prevents an accident because of his conditioned reflexes; hands and feet respond more quickly than thought.

I'm convinced the same thing is true in all other kinds of crisis, too. We react to our conditioning built up of every single decision we've made all our lives; who we have used as our mirrors; as our points of reference. If our slow and reasoned decisions are generally wise, those which have to be made quickly are apt to be wise, too. If our reasoned decisions are foolish, so will be those of the sudden situation.

One of the girls gave this example: a group of men are in the Arctic. One is badly hurt. If the others leave him to get back to safety themselves, he will die. If they stay with him, they will all very likely die before help comes. The reasonable decision, the ethical decision in this situation, she was told, is for the others to leave so that only one man will die.

Everything in me rebels. It was the reasonable decision made once before when Caiaphas said that it is expedient that one man die for the sake of the nation.

What would E. M. Forster think? To leave your friend and save the group is not, after all, the particular. It is the general once again.

We killed one man for the sake of the nation once. Didn't we learn anything?

. . 13 . .

It leads me back to Pope John daring to make a decision without knowing what was going to happen. I hope that I, like E. M. Forster, would choose to stay with my friend, and perhaps die. But I would not need to be able to predict the outcome to make the choice. If one must predict every outcome, then the logical thing *is* to save those you can and leave your friend to die.

Something that happened when we lived in the country helps me here. During our General Store, diaper, and snowsuit years, Hugh did a good deal of lay preaching. He did not talk as a minister or priest but simply as a human being, a father, a man, sharing his thoughts with the members of the congregation. One Sunday he was asked to talk in a church in a nearby town. I could not be with him, because I could not leave the choir; we were doing a difficult anthem, and it wasn't only that I was needed to "conduct." I was needed for moral support—not only by the choir; the anthem was in three sharps at the time when Grandma would occasionally still tackle sharps.

When Hugh came home he was despondent. He had talked about family, about the relationship of parents and children. He had talked from his heart about things important to him and to every parent, and he had felt from the congregation nothing but a wall of blankness. They had sat there politely; they hadn't coughed; but he felt that there had been no response whatsoever.

The next day a car drove up to the store, and a man Hugh had never seen before got out and came in. "Mr. Franklin, I just had to come tell you. I heard you at church yesterday. I'm a contractor just starting out for myself. I work hard, and I'm doing all right, but I've been all tied up in knots. I haven't been able to eat and sleep, and when the kids have asked me questions I've snapped at them, and a couple of times I've had my wife in tears. Yesterday I came home from church and I joked with the kids at the table, and it was the first time we've laughed during a meal in I can't tell you when. Afterwards I helped my girl with her spelling. She's been having a tough time, and I managed to make it make sense to her. Then I went out and played ball with my son. The knot was gone from my stomach, and I slept all night like a baby. I had to come tell you."

But if he hadn't come to tell Hugh, the result would have been the same. If we accept the responsibility of a situation, there is a response, whether we know it or not, and whether it's the response we expect—or want. Perhaps we may be required to die with our friend?

.. 14 ..

Suppose the strange little iceberg that is the human mind (the largest part submerged, ignored, feared) is also likened to a living radio or television set. With our conscious, surface selves we

224

are able to tune in only a very few wave lengths. But there are others, and sometimes in our dreams we will pick up a scene from a distant, unknown, seemingly non-rational channel—but is it non-rational? Or is it in another language, using metaphors and similes with which we are not yet familiar?

"Consciousness expanding" is part of the current jargon. When I was very young and even more naïve than I am now, living alone in Greenwich Village, something in my non-rational mind rejected suggestions made to me by people older and far cleverer than I, that I should sleep with them because such experience was necessary for my development as a writer. The same kind of instinctive non-rational rejection came to me when a young man offered me LSD; he was taking it, and he thought in it to find all the answers. For a moment I was tempted. But I have watched him becoming more and more confused as he uses the drug to try to move more deeply into himself; as he tries to find himself he succeeds only in losing himself. He was talking about his self-searching one day to Will and me as he prepared to take a "trip." Will asked, "But what do you really expect from it?" He answered, "Instant meditation."

We don't hurt ourselves—except aesthetically, which is not to be taken lightly—by drinking instant coffee or eating powdered eggs, but we do hurt ourselves when we try to take short cuts to find out who we are, and what our place in the universe.

Not that I am against consciousness expanding: I want as much of my little iceberg as possible out in the full light of the sun, and I want to be clearly aware of the beautiful country beneath the waters. All forms of art are consciousness expanders, and I am convinced that they will take us further, and more consciously, than drugs. For me, writing is the obvious one. But so is reading the great writers. So is going to a museum, or listening to a Schubert Quartet, or, better still, sitting at the piano and making music, no matter how fumblingly. And so are our dreams. I want to remember them, not so that I can recount them at boring length, but so that I will be less insular, less afraid to travel in foreign lands. We are very foolish if we shrug and patronizingly consider that these voyages are not real.

My husband is automatically suspicious of what is commonly called mysticism, or the supernatural. He is right to be dubious. This is dangerous territory, and to experiment foolishly can lead to death and damnation. I don't understand mysticism, but I do know that the kind of Be-a-Mystic-in-One-Easy-Lesson-in-Contemplation which is becoming fashionable has nothing whatsoever to do with the real thing. I think that one cannot be a mystic consciously any more than one can have integrity or be humble consciously. But there are, indeed, Horatio, more things in heaven and earth than our philosophies can account for. So I send out two messages from the realm where truth has nothing to do with provable fact.

The first message is not very cosmic in importance, but it is definitely outside the bounds of proof.

When I first started as librarian of the Cathedral, I, with Oliver, our old collie, took a route which led up Broadway, then turned east at 110th Street. We would then proceed up either the south or the north side of the street, depending on whether the light was red or green at that point. One morning we were walking up the north side, and Oliver gave a tremendous leap, as though he had been frightened by something, and almost threw me. I didn't pay much attention when the same thing happened the next time, but when it happened a third time, when it happened every time we passed one particular building, I began to wonder. Oliver would either fling to the end of his leash or he would make an elaborate, quivering circle around something I could not see.

I told my husband, the calm humanist, the iconoclast, the reasonable intellectual. Naturally he doubted; he laughed. The next time we were going to dinner with one of our friends at the Cathedral, he took Oliver's leash. Although I hated to see Oliver frightened (I now walked him only up the south side), I found myself wanting something to happen. It did. Oliver nearly threw him.

For over a year Hugh kept testing him; sometimes Oliver would only press, trembling, against Hugh as we walked by. But something always happened; Oliver saw, felt, feared, something that we did not, and whatever this thing was, it was evil.

When I tell this story and friends pooh-pooh, I turn to Hugh for corroboration. "Oh, it happened," he says. "I can't explain it, but it very definitely happened."

.. 15 ..

The second message moves deeper into the ocean.

When I was little we usually visited my maternal grandmother during the summer when she lived at the beach. I called my grandmother Dearma, because I thought that's what all grandmothers were called. The Saint-Gaudens children called old Madame Saint-Gaudens Dearma, and as I look at the snapshots of very small Madeleine with the formidable mother of Augustus Saint-Gaudens, and think of my own grandmother, equally austere and dignified, it seems an oddly familiar name even for a grandchild. Now that I have grandchildren of my own, I understand this total lack of awe rather better.

In any case, I called my magnificent grandmother Dearma, and I loved the house at the beach in a special way. It was there that I was first taken out at night to see stars, and where I first sensed ultimate design in the universe. I've always had a feeling of personal communication with stars, not in the sense of astrology but in the sense of feeling a consciousness which encompasses all the tiny human consciousness on earth and enlarges it.

When we returned to the United States after several years abroad, we went to spend the summer at the beach with Dearma. What I am going to tell happened at summer's end. It was Sunday night. During the day it had been hot and sunny, and friends and relations dropped by to see us and Dearma; we sat on the veranda and rocked, fanned ourselves with palm-leaf fans, and drank cool drinks. It was quiet, and typical of a Southern Sunday. We went early to bed.

While I was getting undressed I had the strange, almost asthmatic feeling of pressure that sometimes comes before a thunderstorm. Thunderstorms are frequent at the beach, but I knew that this oppression did not come from storm. It was a presage of something terrible.

It never occurred to me to tell my parents. I did tell God. My faith was still a child's faith, and still very much my own. My school was Anglican, with chapel morning and evening; I never felt the presence of God very strongly there; I did feel him at night in bed when at last I could be alone in dark and silence. So I prayed to him now: Please, don't let anything terrible happen. Please.

The answer was very clear; not in words, though I am going to have to set it down in words, but in certainty:

Not only was something terrible going to happen, but I now

knew what that something was to be: my grandmother would die that night.

Dearma was in her seventies; her heart was not very good; but there was nothing to indicate imminent death. I was too young to have heard about second sight or pre-vision. I am not at all sure what my parents would have said had I gone in to them. I did not. I prayed and prayed that the answer would be changed, but it was not.

I didn't do much sleeping. I would slide in and out of the shallows of sleep, always on the edge of wakefulness, always listening, waiting. Sometime in the very early hours of the morning I sat up, completely awake, as though I had heard a sudden noise, though I had not. I listened. Nothing. But I knew that this was the time to get my parents. I went to their room and woke them, saying, "Please go in to Dearma."

We went in and she was breathing strangely, her last breaths. She was not conscious; she went to bed and to sleep and died. The doctor came and pronounced her dead. The breathing had stopped; she was very still.

There was no wind. The ocean seemed to be holding its breath.

Coffee, as usual in times of stress, was brewed by somebody. At dawn my mother and I went swimming. I think Father stayed with Dearma.

I remember putting on my bathing suit and walking across the beach with my mother in the strange cool of dawn, totally in communion with her, walking silently into the shallow ocean, into the waves, and into a sunrise more beautiful than any I remember before or since. It was the sunrise which made everything bearable, which helped me to accept that death is a part of life.

There are more things, Horatio. We will never understand them all, not now, not here. But we are foolish to underestimate them, explain them away, pretend they do not exist.

.. 16 ..

So Einstein's calling on the necessity for mystery in the scientist's life did not surprise me. I was rather more startled to discover Freud saying that the two groups of people who defy psychological knowledge are the artists and the saints. None of the rules of psychology hold for them. Thornton Wilder also classed artists and saints together in *Our Town*. After Emily dies she is allowed to come back to earth to relive a day, and she is torn apart by her awareness of all that she has always taken for granted. She asks the stage manager, "Do any human beings ever realize life while they live it?—every, every minute?" And he answers, "No. The saints and poets, maybe—they do, some."

Tallis once told me that a great mathematician said, "Mathematics is the conscious setting aside of facts until we have found a conclusion." Einstein's own work demonstrates his words on the mysterious; he did not come to his theories by working them out consciously; rather, he took enormous leaps, like Nureyev defying gravity, and there were his conclusions waiting for him, out in the realm of the mysterious. After that he had to go back and get it all worked out mathematically.

Copernicus discovered that the earth revolves around the sun in the same mysterious way the great artist works. Mathematically, it *can* be proved that the sun, the planets, the stars, all revolve around our earth, that we *are* the center of the universe. But this was not an artistically beautiful equation, and this bothered Copernicus. He didn't have any idea that he was going to discover that we revolve around a middle-sized sun in a back-wash of our particular galaxy; what he was interested in was making a mathematically elegant equation. He did, and as a result the entire theory of the universe changed; it shook some people's belief in God—it's rather nice to think that the universe was created entirely for the benefit of mankind. For others this discovery, and all the discoveries of science, strengthens faith in God's glory and mystery.

The great astronomer, Tycho Brahe, put on his court robes before going to his telescope. The artist should have the same reverence in approaching his work. Something happens in his life, in the world around him, which is the equivalent of an ignoble mathematical equation. So he "puts on his court robes" and sometimes, as a result, we get a *House of Atreus,* or a *Dr. Faustus,* or a *Wuthering Heights;* or, I venture to say, a *Wind in the Willows,* or a *Sleeping Beauty,* or an *Alice Through the Looking Glass.*

Why do we try to cut down the forests and remove the brambles and thorny roses of this radiant land?

One of my English aunts now lives in an ancient, rheumatism-producing castle in Scotland, because it has been in her husband's family since before the Norman Conquest. But she lived for many years in Kenya, where, after her first husband's death, she managed his vast estate singlehanded. On one of her rare trips to the United States she was staying in New York, at the Hotel Plaza. And she was puzzled because she was wakened, every morning, by the roaring of the lions, exactly as though she were still in Kenya. Lions on the island of Manhattan? It seemed most unlikely, and she mentioned it to a friend. The friend became most agitated over my Aunt Alexandra's mental health, and insisted on setting up an appointment with a well-known psychiatrist who, when Alexandra's symptom was

described, felt that it was urgent that she see him at once. Fortunately, before the appointment, Alexandra mentioned hearing
lions at dawn to another friend, who laughed and said, "Of
course. You're hearing the lions in the Central Park Zoo. It's
just across from the Plaza."

I wish we didn't try to turn real lions into imaginary ones.
The lions are not imaginary. They are real. I have experienced
a lot of lions in my lifetime, and these encounters are what I
write about, and why I write as a storyteller: it's the best way to
make the lions visible. But the lions must be those of my own
experience. Our projecting from the tangible present into the
"what if" of the imagination must be within the boundaries of
our own journeying.

.. 17 ..

When I do something wrong I tend to alibi, to make excuses,
blame someone else. Until I can accept whatever it is that I
have done, I am only widening the gap between my real and my
ontological self, and I am thus excluding myself so that I begin
to think that I am unforgivable.

We need to be forgiven:

to be forgiven in this time when fish are dying in our rivers;
in this time of poison gas dumped on the ocean floor and in the
less and less breathable air of our cities, of children starving;
being burned to death in wars which stumble on; being at-
tacked by rats in their cribs . . .

we need to be forgiven in this grey atmosphere which clogs
the lungs so that we cannot breathe, and breathless, spiritless,
can no longer discern what is right and what is wrong, what is

our right hand and what is our left, what is justice and what tyranny, what is life and what is death.

I heard a man of brilliance cry out that God has withdrawn from nations when they have turned from Him, and surely we are a stiff-necked people; why should He not withdraw?

But then I remember Jonah accusing God of overlenience, of foolishness, mercy, and compassion.

We desperately need the foolishness of God.

.. 18 ..

During my last year in boarding school I had attained the elevated position of Head of School; I was editor of the yearbook and literary magazine, played leading roles in the school plays. I had finally made it. I also had all the answers, theologically speaking. I went, with all the other Episcopalians in the school, to the Episcopal church on Sunday; it bored me totally, and it was then that I picked up the habit of writing poetry during sermons. When it came to the General Confession in Morning Prayer I was, with proper humility, willing to concede that I occasionally left undone a few things which I ought to have done (I was, after all, very busy), and I occasionally did a few things which I ought not to have done (I was, after all, not "pi"); but I was not willing to say that I was a miserable offender and that there was no health in me.

It's a stage we all go through; it takes a certain amount of living to strike the strange balance between the two errors either of regarding ourselves as unforgivable or as not needing forgiveness.

During the Crosswicks years when the children were little, a new hymnal was put out for the Congregational church. In the back is a section of prayers, and it includes the General Confession from the Book of Common Prayer. It is an interesting commentary on human nature in this confused century that precisely those words which I could not, would not say as an adolescent were deleted from the Congregational prayers.

By that time, in the midst of my fumbling agnosticism, it had become very clear to me that I *was* a miserable offender, and that there was very little health in me. I wasn't falling into that peculiar trap of *hubris* which tempts one into thinking that one is sinfuler than thou. If I never got through a day when I didn't do at least one thing I regretted, this was assuredly true of everybody else I knew. Perhaps my friends were not tempted, as I was, to do a Gauguin, but they had their own major temptations. Perhaps their sins of omission were less in the housewifely area than mine, but surely they had their own equivalent. I was rather upset by the mutilation of the Confession.

"It's all right to think you can be virtuous if you try just a little harder when you're an adolescent," I told Quinn, "but I don't like having the church behave like an adolescent."

When we moved back to New York a series of those noncoincidences started me back into the church in which I was born, the church of John Donne, Lancelot Andrewes, Shakespeare. A friend of Alan's, doing his Ph.D. in seventeenth-century English literature, became an Anglican, saying that one can hardly spend so much time with all these people without sharing their beliefs. When, shortly after our return, the Episcopal church put out a trial liturgy, I was unhappy with it for two major reasons: it was not worded in the best language of which we are capable; and it made the confession before receiving communion optional.

We haven't done a very good job of righting the wrongs of

our parents or our peers, my generation. We can't say to our children, here is a green and peaceful world we have prepared for you and your children: enjoy it. We can offer them only war and pollution and senility. And this is the time we decide, in our churches, that we're so virtuous we don't need to be forgiven: symbolically, iconically forgiven.

If the Lord's table is the prototype of the family table, then, if I think in terms of the family table, I know that I cannot sit down to bread and wine until I've said I'm sorry, until reparations have been made, relations restored. When one of our children had done something particularly unworthy, if it had come out into the open before dinner, if there had been an "I'm sorry," and there had been acceptance, and love, then would follow the happiest dinner possible, full of laughter and fun. If there was something still hidden; if one child, or as sometimes happens, one parent, was out of joint with the family and the world, that would destroy the atmosphere of the whole meal.

What is true of the family table is, in another sense, true of the conjugal bed. Twin beds make no sense to me. I can understand an occasional need for a separate room, but not separate beds. If a man and wife get into bed together it is very difficult to stay mad. Both Hugh and I have tried, and it hasn't worked. The touch of a hand is enough to dissolve me into tenderness; the touch of a cold foot enough to dissolve me into laughter. One way or another, reparation is made, relations restored, love returned.

Only a human being can say *I'm sorry. Forgive me.* This is part of our particularity. It is part of what makes us capable of tears, capable of laughter.

I've mentioned Dana, Dana Catherine de Ruiz, who has been a member of the Crosswicks family for so long that I cannot remember a time when she has not been a bright and beautiful part of it. We knew her first as a girl in the grade above Josephine at school. The two of them were pleasant acquaintances but became real friends one summer when they were both on the same job, were both overworked, and fled together to sit in an ancient cemetery for a small respite. If you will think about it, there are not many people with whom you can sit on a tombstone and be at peace.

One day as we were walking home down the lane, Dana said, "I don't think of you as my godmother. I think of you as my godfriend." Surely that is the right description of our relationship. Dana may be young enough to be my daughter in chronology; in eternity she is considerably older than I am. There is nothing we don't talk about, and we share a great many friends —but since our friends range in age from one year to ninety, that's not as odd as it may sound.

Dana knows that the idea of a Little Gidding, that community of people in England three and a half centuries ago, working together, suffering together, rejoicing together, never losing an awareness of their responsibility to the entire world, is immensely appealing to me. I certainly understand, in my blood and bones, the need young people today have to group together in "communes," to try to bind up in community the wounds of our present fragmentation. This is what I am groping towards myself, and what I find tangible in the summer in our Crosswicks family, and in the winter in the family of the Cathedral Close.

Walking down the lane through the shifting shadows of the trees, I mentioned longingly to Dana my desire to live, eventually, in a Little Gidding kind of community, and she said calmly, "You do."

Yes. Wherever there is unity in diversity, then we are free to be ourselves; it cannot be done in isolation; we need each other.

Before we eat dinner at night we all join hands around the table, and, for me, this circle of love is the visible symbol of all I hope for, and all that Dana meant.

..20..

One of the things I am most grateful for is my very lack of ability as a pastry cook. A decade ago when we first moved back to New York from Crosswicks, we put our children in a nearby school, St. Hilda's and St. Hugh's. We did some soul-searching over this, because we feel strongly about the value of the American public-school system and we wanted to be part of it. My husband went through the Tulsa public schools. I, growing up in New York and Europe, went only to private or independent schools. I hope it's because I was for so long in school abroad that I know so little about American geography. When Hugh and I were in a play in Chicago, the stage manager came in to the theatre with her dog, saying that they had had such a lovely walk by the lake. "Oh, did you walk around it?" I asked.

I was given a geography book for Christmas.

Hugh and I were married in Chicago during the run of another play—we met in *The Cherry Orchard* and married in *The Joyous Season*, and after the play closed we bought a very second-hand car and set off to see his family in Oklahoma, and mine in the South. I remember two things about the car: the license plates for Illinois in 1946 were made of soybeans; and there was something wrong with the gearshift; it kept slipping back into neutral. We drove through the Ozarks with one hand holding the recalcitrant gearshift in high.

I had never been west of Chicago, and I knew nothing about Oklahoma. I blush to report that I asked Hugh if the streets of Tulsa were paved. Granted, he was leading me on. It was when he told me that his mother put on shoes to go to church that I realized that I was being had.

But it isn't fair to blame independent school education. And the public school in our neighborhood when we returned to the city was one of the worst in New York. We were, and are, more than grateful for St. Hilda's and St. Hugh's—and of course, with a name like St. Hugh, it was obviously the place for us.

One day the children came home with the usual mimeographed petition for a cake for the bazaar. They were new at the school and they wanted their mother to do the right thing. "Please, Mother." So I baked a cake.

I'm as bad at cakes as I am at cherry pies. The last cherry pie I made was shortly after we were married and Hugh had some people from the Theatre Guild in for dinner, and I was determined to impress them with my wifely virtues. When it was time for dessert I didn't think the pie crust was brown enough, so I put it under the broiler. We had to get the fire extinguisher.

So I made a cake for my children's sake. It tasted delicious. But it didn't look the way it tasted. It was lopsided: a mess. I wrote the headmistress a note which ran more or less like this: "I tried. I baked a cake. Because my family loves me, they will eat it. But it is obvious that this is not the way in which I can be of use to the school. Is there anything else I could do, more in line with my talents? Is there a play we could help with, or anything like that?"

238

Within a few days Hugh and I found that we were directing the Christmas pageant, with the entire Cathedral of St. John the Divine as our stage: Mr. and Mrs. Max Reinhardt. It's quite something to see the three kings march in their glorious costumes the length of two city blocks.

If I had been able to bake that cake for the school cake sale I might still be in darkness. Father Anthony (I speak of him so casually: he is Metropolitan of Surozh and Exarch of the Russian Patriarchal in Western Europe) said last spring that it is good to have turned to God as he did, as I did, after a time of darkness, because then one truly knows what it is like to be dead, and now to be alive.

Hugh and I first ran into Canon Tallis when we were directing the pageant at the Cathedral, after my cake-baking fiasco. Ran into is right. We clashed. He did not like vast quantities of school children in the Cathedral during Advent, that austere time of eschatology, reenacting the Christmas story out of chronology. He bristled when he saw us. We bristled when we saw him. We could conceive of no reason why the pageant wasn't the most important thing in the world, why he didn't put at our disposal all the facilities of the Cathedral.

Later, when I knew him better, I explained to him, passionately, that the chronology of the pageant wasn't really what was important; Christmas is an arbitrary date anyhow; the important thing was that the children should have some idea of Christmas beyond street-corner Santa Clauses and loudspeakers braying out Christmas carols. "Don't you understand that many of them won't have any Christmas otherwise? They won't even go to church. If it's not to be a blasphemy they'll have to have it here, now, before the school vacation begins, out of chronology —but in real time."

Thus Madeleine the agnostic.

But we did, after that, have all the cooperation possible from the Cathedral staff.

Later on I went to Canon Tallis, almost by accident, when I was in trouble. I'd made an appointment with another canon at the Cathedral, and his secretary forgot to put the appointment in his book. He was full of apologies, but had to be away, so couldn't see me later, and suggested Tallis. Canon Tallis was the last person I wanted to see. Something told me that it would either work magnificently or be totally horrible.

It worked magnificently.

It wasn't that my problem was solved but that I had help in bearing it. I also told him all my intellectual doubts, my total incredulity about the incarnation; the idea that God could pitch his tent among men was absurd. Of course! It still is.

I had talked with several Congregational minister friends about my intellectual doubts. I was eager to be converted—I didn't like atheism or agnosticism; I was by then well aware that I am not self-sufficient, that I needed the dimension of transcendence. They were eager to convert me. But they explained everything. For every question I asked, they had an answer. They tried to reach me through my mind.

First of all, my mind is not that good. I'm not stupid; I did graduate from Smith with honors. But I am, basically, not an intellectual. Nevertheless, I knew that I could not throw away my mind, and it was not the discoveries of science that bothered me. On the contrary. The book I read during this period which brought me closest to God was one that never mentioned God, *The Limitations of Science,* by J. W. N. Sullivan.

My minister friends gave me all kinds of theological books to read, mostly by German theologians. The more I read, the further I was shoved away from any kind of acceptance. I would read logical explanations of the totally mysterious scandal of particularity and think: if I have to believe all this bunk, then Christianity is not for me. One line in the Book of Common Prayer made sense to me: *the mystery of the word made flesh.* If only my friends would admit that it *was* a mystery, and stop giving me explanations! I wrote in my journal: "I talk to people—oh, people I respect, people I like—and yet I never feel any sense of terrific excitement in their own lives about Jesus, in the way that the early Christians must have been excited so that they were transfigured by Jesus. In no one, no one, no matter how loudly they talk about salvation being possible only through Jesus, do I find this great thing *showing* in them, glowing in them, lighting their lives, as it must if it is to make any sense today at all." I was, I am sure, less than fair; nevertheless that was what reasonable explanations did to me.

Canon Tallis did not explain anything. He listened to my doubts in silence. I think he thought they were really very unimportant. As far as my specific, daily problems were concerned, I found that I could take them more lightly, could laugh more easily.

Then spring came. Hugh was away with the tour of *Luther.* He'd had a fine time playing Cardinal Cajetan on Broadway, and we felt that he should go on tour. But all kinds of things happened that spring. Bion, eleven, started running a high fever, for which no explanation could be found. At the hospital the doctor assured me that there was a physical cause, and they would go on testing until they found it. For forty-eight hours I lived with the knowledge that the doctor thought that Bion had cancer of the liver. He had been talking to me in abstruse medical terms, but one of my closest friends is a doctor, and I more or less went through medical school with her, and suddenly the doctor looked at me and said, "Do you know what I am talking about?"

"Yes. I'm afraid I do."

"We're re-testing, and I'll call you as soon as the results are in."

Hugh and I were trying not to phone each other too often; we called about every three days. He would be phoning the evening that we would know the results. By shortly after six, when Hugh usually called, I had not heard anything. Then the phone rang, and I dreaded telling Hugh what we feared; there was never any question of keeping it from him; he'd hear it in my voice. But it was not Hugh, it was the doctor, and it was not cancer.

Then Hugh's father died, and he had to fly from Chicago to Tulsa for the funeral. He called me from Chicago before leaving; I already knew, because I had talked to his sister that morning. While Hugh and I were talking, I could hear his voice break, and he said in astonishment, "Isn't it extraordinary, this is the first time I've felt anything about Dad, talking to you." But of course we both knew that it wasn't extraordinary at all.

Then happy news. Josephine was to be salutatorian of her class, graduating at sixteen. We were joyful and proud. But Hugh couldn't come for graduation, because he had taken time off from the play for his father's funeral. And Bion was still in the hospital.

Then something happened, something so wounding that it cannot possibly be written down. Think of two of the people you love most in the world; think of a situation in which both are agonizingly hurt and you are powerless to do anything to help. It is far easier to bear pain for ourselves than for those we love, especially when part of it is that we cannot share the pain but must stand by, unable to alleviate it.

Canon Tallis hardly knew us at all, then. But he stepped in. What he did is involved with all that I cannot write. The point right now is that this was the moment of light for me, because it was an act of love, Love made visible.

And that did it. Possibly nothing he could have done for me, myself, would have illuminated the world for me as did this act of love towards those I love. Because of this love, this particular (never general) Christian love, my intellectual reservations no longer made the least difference. I had seen love in action, and that was all the proof I needed.

. . 21 . .

There is no more beautiful witness to the mystery of the word made flesh than a baby's naked body. I remember with sensory clarity sitting with one of my babies on my lap and running my hand over the incredibly pure smoothness of the bare back and thinking that any mother, holding her child thus, must have at least an echo of what it is like to be Mary; that in touching the particular created matter, flesh, of our child, we are touching the Incarnation. Alan, holding his daughter on his lap, running his hand over her bare back with the same tactile appreciation with which I had touched my children, made a similar remark.

Once, when I was in the hospital, the smooth and beautiful white back of the woman in the bed next to mine, a young woman dying of cancer, was a stabbing and bitter reminder of the ultimate end of all matter.

But not just our human bodies: all matter: the stars in their courses: everything: the end of time.

Meanwhile we are in time, and the flesh is to be honored. At all ages. For me, this summer, this has been made clear in a threefold way: I have fed, bathed, played pat-a-cake with my grandbabies. In the night when I wake up, as I usually do, I always reach out with a foot, a hand, to touch my husband's body; I go back to sleep with my hand on his warm flesh. And my mother is almost ninety and preparing to move into a different country. I do not understand the mysteries of the flesh, but I know that we must not be afraid to reach out to each other, to hold hands, to touch.

In our bedroom there is a large old rocking chair which was in the attic of Crosswicks when we bought it. It seems to have been made especially for mothers and babies. I have sat in it and nursed my babe in the middle of the night. I have sung innumerable lullabies from it. When Hugh was in *Medea*, which was sent overseas in 1951 by the State Department, I sat in the rocking chair, carrying his child within me and holding our first-born in my arms, singing all the old lullabies, but especially *Sweet and Low* because of "over the Western sea," and "Bring him again to me."

This summer I sit in the rocking chair and rock and sing with one or other of my granddaughters. I sing the same songs I sang all those years ago. It feels utterly right. Natural. The same.

But it isn't the same. I may be holding a baby just as I used to hold a baby, but chronology has done many things in the intervening years, to the world, to our country, to my children, to me. I may feel, rocking a small, loving body, no older than I felt rocking that body's mother. But I am older bodily; my energy span is not as long as it used to be; at night my limbs ache with fatigue; my eyes are even older than the rest of me. It is going to seem very early—it is going to *be* very early—when the babies wake up: Alan, Josephine, Cynthia, and I take turns getting up and going downstairs with them, giving them breakfast, making the coffee. Is it my turn again so quickly?

Chronology: the word about the measurable passage of time, although its duration varies: how long is a toothache? how long is standing in line at the supermarket? how long is a tramp through the fields with the dogs? or dinner with friends, or a sunset, or the birth of a baby?

Chronology, the time which changes things, makes them grow older, wears them out, and manages to dispose of them, chronologically, forever.

Thank God there is kairos, too: again the Greeks were wiser than we are. They had two words for time: *chronos* and *kairos.*

Kairos is not measurable. Kairos is ontological. In kairos we *are,* we are fully in isness, not negatively, as Sartre saw the isness of the oak tree, but fully, wholly, positively. Kairos can sometimes enter, penetrate, break through chronos: the child at play, the painter at his easel, Serkin playing the *Appassionata,* are in kairos. The saint at prayer, friends around the dinner table, the mother reaching out her arms for her newborn baby, are in kairos. The bush, the burning bush, is in kairos, not any burning bush, but the very particular burning bush before which Moses removed his shoes; the bush I pass on my way to the brook. In kairos that part of us which is not consumed in the burning is wholly awake. We too often let it fall asleep, not as the baby in my arms droops into sleepiness, but dully, blunt-ingly.

I sit in the rocking chair with a baby in my arms, and I am in both kairos and chronos. In chronos I may be nothing more than some cybernetic salad on the bottom left-hand corner of a check; or my social-security number; or my passport number. In kairos I am known by name: Madeleine.

The baby doesn't know about chronos yet.

I'm off to the brook again. Summer is almost over; the golden rod is aflame. The bush burns with the red of autumn. The family has scattered, is scattering, to England, Mexico, Florida, California, to the big house across the lane and up the road. I've already started moving things back to New York. We are having a deep, gentle, September rain, which the land, the trees, the brook need thirstily. Yesterday I waded downstream for a long time, wet from the waters of the brook itself, from the rain, from the drops shaking from the leaves as I pushed under, over, through the overhanging trees.

The brook, the bush, the sun-warmed rock, as in the song, have seen, felt, touched, healed me.

Gregory of Nyssa points out that Moses's vision of God began with the light, with the visible burning bush, the bush which was bright with fire and was not consumed; but afterwards, God spoke to him in a cloud. After the glory which could be seen with human eyes, he began to see the glory which is beyond and after light.

The shadows are deepening all around us. Now is the time when we must begin to see our world and ourselves in a different way.

MADELEINE L'ENGLE,

who has "written stories ever since I was old enough to hold a pencil," has interspersed her writing and teaching career with raising three children, maintaining a big, old apartment in New York and a farmhouse of charming confusion in Connecticut which is called "Crosswicks."

Author photo by Beverly Hall

THE CROSSWICKS JOURNAL

BOOK 1
A Circle of Quiet

"The 'Circle of Quiet' is her personal place of retreat near a brook, a ten-minute walk from their country home. This volume is a sharing of her inner life shaped primarily from materials in her journals."—*Provident Book Finder*

BOOK 2
The Summer of the Great-grandmother

". . . an almost taboo subject of senility and old age. This book is a somewhat unconventional memoir of a much-loved parent. But it is also a book concerned with the aged and the dying—a book that takes a look at many of the attitudes and values in today's society." —*Associated Press*

BOOK 3
The Irrational Season

"It's hard to imagine readers failing to get a spiritual lift from *The Irrational Season* . . . the book is especially valuable, for it's an exploration of L'Engle's life as a professional woman, wife, mother, and grandmother." —*Publishers' Weekly*

THE SEABURY PRESS • NEW YORK